CW01197170

1 MONTH OF FREE READING

at

www.ForgottenBooks.com

By purchasing this book you are eligible for one month membership to ForgottenBooks.com, giving you unlimited access to our entire collection of over 1,000,000 titles via our web site and mobile apps.

To claim your free month visit: www.forgottenbooks.com/free892359

* Offer is valid for 45 days from date of purchase. Terms and conditions apply.

ISBN 978-0-265-80661-6
PIBN 10892359

This book is a reproduction of an important historical work. Forgotten Books uses state-of-the-art technology to digitally reconstruct the work, preserving the original format whilst repairing imperfections present in the aged copy. In rare cases, an imperfection in the original, such as a blemish or missing page, may be replicated in our edition. We do, however, repair the vast majority of imperfections successfully; any imperfections that remain are intentionally left to preserve the state of such historical works.

Forgotten Books is a registered trademark of FB &c Ltd.
Copyright © 2018 FB &c Ltd.
FB &c Ltd, Dalton House, 60 Windsor Avenue, London, SW19 2RR.
Company number 08720141. Registered in England and Wales.

For support please visit www.forgottenbooks.com

THE

HISTORICAL COLLECTIONS

OF THE

TOPSFIELD HISTORICAL SOCIETY

VOL. X

1905

TOPSFIELD, MASS.

Published by the Society

1905

GEORGE FRANCIS DOW

Editor

THE MERRILL PRESS
𝔗𝔬𝔭𝔰𝔣𝔦𝔢𝔩𝔡
MASS

CONTENTS.

REGISTER OF BAPTISMS, MARRIAGES, AND BIRTHS AT ST. MARGARET'S, TOPPESFIELD, ENG., 1559–1650, *Illustrated*,	1
ELEGY ON THE DEATH OF BENJAMIN KIMBALL, 1775, BY REV. JOHN CLEAVELAND,	68
SMITH FAMILY LETTERS,	74
REMINISCENCES OF REV. ASAHEL HUNTINGTON,	78
LETTER FROM JOHN PEABODY, 1811,	81
REVOLUTIONARY WAR RECORDS,	83
PEABODY–BATCHELDER–YOUNG HOUSE, BY JOHN H. TOWNE, *Illustrated*,	84
BOYD–PEABODY–WATERS HOUSE, BY JOHN H. TOWNE, *Illustrated*,	86
PATRIOTIC SONG, COMPOSED BY SETH PEABODY,	88
INSCRIPTIONS FROM LAKE FAMILY BURYING-GROUND,	90
FRANCIS PEABODY'S WILL, 1698,	91
NEWSPAPER ITEMS, 1805–1815, COPIED BY GEORGE FRANCIS DOW,	98
TOPSFIELD VITAL STATISTICS, 1903,	137
CHRONOLOGY OF EVENTS, 1903,	140
BUILDINGS CONSTRUCTED, 1903,	140
TOPSFIELD VITAL STATISTICS, 1904,	141
CHRONOLOGY OF EVENTS, 1904,	144
BUILDINGS CONSTRUCTED, 1904,	144
INDEX TO TOPSFIELD HISTORICAL COLLECTIONS, VOLS. I–X,	145

THE REGISTER OF BAPTISMS, MARRIAGES AND BURIALS, AT ST. MARGARET'S TOPPESFIELD, ENGLAND, 1559–1650.

TRANSCRIBED BY REV. H. B. BARNES, RECTOR.

On the fly leaf of the Register appears the following:

> When Advent Clime to take his time,
>   then out goes wedding tide,
> Like Artillary, in Comes Hillary,
>   with weddings at his side.
> Septuagint takes the next hint,
>   and bids them next adewe,
> But Ester Mass, wth eight days pass,
>   thou mayst get wedd anewe.
> Rogation did yt last forbid,
>   & bid thee pray instedd,
> But Trinity gives liberty,
>   to make a marriag bedd.
>
> Conjugium Adventus tollit Hilarius relaxat
> Septuagesima vetat sed pascæ octava reducit
> Rogamen vetitat, commendit trina potestas.

NOTE: For a description of St. Margaret's Church and a list of its rectors, together with some account of Toppesfield Parish, see Topsfield Historical Collections, Vol. VI, pp. 107–136.

Advent wils the to conteine
But Hilary sets the free again,
Septuagesima saies the nay
But Eight from Easter saies thou may.
Rogation bids the yet to tarrie
But Trinity gives the leáve to marrie.

Duodecim Impedimenta matrimonii juxta Canonistas scil:

1.	2.	3.	4.	5.
Error.	conditio.	votum.	cognatio.	crimen.
6.	7.	8.	9.	10.
Cultus disparitas.	vis.	ordo.	legamen.	honestas.
11.		12.		
Si sis affinis.		si forte coire nequibis.		

On the reverse of the fly leaf is written:

Toppsfield steple fell downe
July the forth day 1689
and five beles and the little
bel broke all to peeceis

BAPTISMS.

[1]
1559　Anne Humfrye the daughter of John Humfrye was baptized the 24th. day of februarie in the yeere of o^r L. God 1559.
　　　John, s. Thomas Webbe, 12th. March.
1560　Joane, d. Richard Yeldam, 31 March.
　　　Margarete, d. John Purkis, 31 March.
　　　John, s. Thomas Pollard, 7 April.
　　　Henrie, s. James Edward, 21 April.
　　　Elizabeth, d. John Hwes, 26 May.
　　　John, s. Henrie Reade, 9 June.
　　　William, s. Thomas Cracherood, 16 June.
　　　William, s. John Plomb, 28 Julie.
　　　John, s. Henrie Thetford, 1st. November.
　　　Thomas, s. Henrie Smith, 22 November.
　　　Henrie, s. John Bust, 26 September.
　　　Anne, d. Thomas Spiltimber, 22 Januarie.
　　　Anne, d. Thomas Greene, 23 Februarie.
　　　Henrie, s. John Humfrie, 2 March.
1561　William, s. William Edward, 13 April.
　　　John, s. John Underod, 7 September.
　　　Anne, d. Richarde Motte, 5 October.
　　　Elizabeth, d. Thomas Cracherood, 2 November.
　　　Henrie, s. Henrie Snellocke, 14 December.
　　　Rose, d. Richard Gipps, 26 December.

NOTE: The folios of the original volume are indicated by the figures enclosed within brackets. The first baptism is copied in the exact form of the original entry. The following records of baptism are printed in condensed form, the unnecessary verbiage having been omitted.

(3)

Robert, s. Thomas Maryet, 18 Januarie.
William, s. William Odell, 1 Februarie.
Richard, s. William Bateman, 24 Februarie.
Nicholas, s. Nicholas Alowe, last day of Februarie.
Alice, d. Henrie Cante, 8 March.
Katherine, d. Richard Gipps, 16 March.
John, s. John Humfrie, 22 March.

1562 Thomas, s. Christopher Fiche, 31 March.
Alice, d. William Addams, 26 Julie.
Thomas, s. Henrie Thetford, 19 Julie.
Thomas, s. Richard Yeldam, 13 September.
Matthew, s. William Edward, 17 Januarie.
Ann, d. Michael Tongue, 17 Januarie.
Anne, d. John Hwes, 10 Februarie.
Alyce, d. Richard Mott, 6 March.
Elizabeth, d. Henrie Snellocke, 6 March.
Elizabeth, d. John Edward, 6 March.

[2] Barbara, d. Thomas Cracherood, 6 April.
1563 Edward, s. John Coosen, 20 May.
William, s. John Humfrie, 6 April.
Margarete Tittrell, 28th. August.
Anne Fitche, 28th August.
Thomas Greene, 28th August.
Alice Edward, 29th August.
Cicely Cooke, 29 September.
Elizabeth Underwodde, 15 October.
Henrie Smith, 30 October.
Margarete Adams, 14 November.
Joane Gridlye, 2 December.
Joane Thetforde, 22 Januarie.
Elizabeth Chote, 4 March.
Marie Powell, 4 March.
Pleasant Cirke, 23 March.

1564 Barbara, d. William Buttall, 23 April.
Richard, s. Thomas Spiltimber, last day of April.
Barbara, d. Michael Tongue, 28 May.
Thomas, s. John Plombe, 30 Julie.
ffrances, d. Thomas Cracherood, 17 August.
John, s. John Rizing, 24 September.
Richard, s. Richard Yeldam, 20 September.

REGISTER. — BAPTISMS.

        Thomas, s. John Humfrie, 25 October.
        Barbara, d. Thomas Maryet, 12 November.
        Rose, d. Robert Edward, 10 December.
        Henrie, s. Henrie Reade, 28 December.
        Anne, d. Thomas Gridlie, 1 Januarie.
        Anne Hibys, d. Thomas Hibys, 5 Februarie.
        ffrancis, s. John Auger, 24 Februarie.
        Thomas. s. Thomas Pollard 11 March.
1565 Margerie, d. Thomas Webb, 8 April.
        Elizabeth, d. William Edward, 18 April.
        Henrie, s. Henrie Harrington, 19th May.
        Margarete, d. William Tailor, 20 May.
        John, s. Thomas Adcocke, 10th June.
        Elizabeth, d. Richard Gipps, 10 June.
        Simon, s. Thomas Greene, 20 June.
        Thomas, s. John Coozin, 28 Julie.
        ffrances, d. John Hwes, 28 Julie.
        Robert, s. Thomas Edward, 19 August.
[3]   Margarete, d. John Underwode, 19 August.
        Anne Mott, d. William Mott, 29 September.
        John, s. Christopher Fitch, 4 October.
        Elizabeth, d. Steven Tytrill, 7 October.
        Henry, s. Richard Mott, 14 October.
        Richard, s. Richard Yeldam, 11 November.
        Anne, d. Henrie Snellocke, 25 November.
        William, s. Michael Tongue, 21 December.
        Henrie, s. Henrie Thetford, 13 Januarie.
        ffrances, d. John Plomb, 14 Januarie.
        Richard, s. Henrie Smithe, 8 March.
        Alyce, d. John Cirke, 11 March.
1566 William, s. Robert Edward, last day of March, 1566.
        William, s. Thomas Mante, 2 April.
        Elizabeth, d. Hugh Rawlin, 16 June.
        William, s. William Butcher, 21 Julie.
        Alice, d. William Buttell, 13 September.
        Thomas, s. John Plomb, 10 November.
        Marie, d. William Taylor, 10 November.
        Barbara, d. Thomas Spiltimber, 28 December.
        Rose, d. William Edward, 9 Februarie.
        Anne, d. Ellen Peacock, 9th March, 1566, baseborn.

Barbara, d. John Humfrie, 18 March.
Elizabeth, d. John Coozin, 20 March.
1567 Richard, s. Steven Tittrill, 30 March.
Agnes, d. Richard Yeldam, 10 April.
Katherine, d. Thomas Hybys, 13 April.
William, s. William Browne, 20 April.
Alyce and ffrances, daughters of Michael Tongue, 24 April.
Joane, d. William Butcher, 15 June.
Briggite, d. Hugh Rawling, 16 Julie.
Richard, s. John Underwood, 3 August.
Elizabeth, d. Richard Perrie, 3 August.
Nicholas, s. Henrie Reade, 4 August.
Elizabeth, d. John Auger, 6 August.
Alyce, d. Henrie Snellock, 7 August.
Elizabeth, d. Thomas Pollard, 24 Sept.
Anne, d. John Plomb, 19 October.
Elizabeth & Jone, daughters of Thomas Adcocke, 2 November.
Richard, s. Christopher ffitch, 18 November.
Elizabeth, d. Henrie Smith, 1 Februarie.
Richard, s. Henrie Thetford, 15 Februarie.
Joane, d. Richard Hulle, 17 Februarie.
John, s. William Mott, 11 March.

[4]
1568 Barbara, d. Thomas Greene, 7th. April.
Cicely, d. Richard Motte, last day of April.
Margerie, d. John Mortemer, 2 Julie.
William, s. William Butcher, 5 August.
William, s. William Buttall, 3 October.
William, s. Richard Yeldam, 3 October.
Marie, d. Nicholas Waede, 24 October.
Agnes, d. John Underwode, 25 October.
Christopher, s. Henrie Snellocke, 15 Januarie.
Thomas, s. Hugh Rawlings, 6 Februarie.
William, s. Thomas Hybys, 24 Februarie.
Rose, d. John Cirke, 27 Februarie.
Henrie, s. Henrie Biggs, 13 March.
1569 Richard, s. William Edward, 28 March.
Elizabeth, d. Henrie Thetford, 29 May.

Ellin, d. John Humfrie, 12 June.
John, s. John Harrington, 27 Julie.
Thomas, s. Robert Edward, 2 August.
Henrie, s. Thomas Spiltymber, 2 October.
Rosanna, d. Edward Richardson, 25 November.
Ellin, d. William Tongue, 22 Januarie.
Elizabeth, d. Thomas Maye, 1 Februarie.
Margaret, d. Thomas Pollerd, 19 Februarie.
William, s. Thomas Greene, 6 March.

1570 William, s. Richard Perrye, 25 March.
Margarie, d. Richard Gipps, 25 April.
Edward, s. Robert Turner, last day April.
Elizabeth, d. saide Robert Turner, last day April.
ffrancis, s. Henrie Snellocke, 26 June.
Emily, d. Rose Plomb, widowe, 8th Julie.
Anne, d. Henrie Smith, 13 August.
Alice, d. John Underwode, 8 October.
Richard, s. Richard Motte, 12 November.
Samuel, s. William Edward, 25 December.
Edward, s. Christopher Fitch, 26 December.
Joyce, d. saide Christopher Fitch, 26 December.
Matthew, s. William Butcher, of Gaynsfords, 1st Januarie.
John, s. John Auger, 14 Januarie.

1571 Henrie, s. Thomas Maye, 6 April.
Alice, d. William Butcher, the thetcher, 6 May.
Marie, d. Henrie Thetford, 20 June.
Robert, s. Robert Aldreade, 12 August.

[5] John, s. Robert Edward, 25 August.
Edward, s. John Humfrie, 2 September.
William, s. Hugh Rawlinge, 7 September.
Joane, d. John Cirke, 18 November.
Edward, s. Edward Richardson, 14 December.
Dorcas, d. Henrie Snellocke, 14 Februarie.

1572 Thomas, s. Thomas Browne, 25 March.
Elizabeth, d. John Buttall, 20 April.
Rose, d. Thomas Spiltimber, 1 May.
Marie, d. Henrie Bigge, 10 August.
Joane, d. John Hamont, 19 September.
Dorcas, d. John Humfrie, 24 September.

Marie, d. William Buttall, 15 October.
Edward, s. Thomas Pollard, 4 Januarie.
Robert, s. William Edward, 11 Januarie.
Elizabeth, d. William Edward, 11 Januarie.
Robert, s. Robert Flowere, 18 Januarie.
Marie, d. Thomas Cracherood, sen., 10 Februarie.

1573 Margarie, d. Henrie Thetford, 25 March.
Phyllis, d. Richard Eeveryde.
Marie, d. Richard Motte, 30 August.
Susan, d. John Auger, 6 September.
Richard, s. Paul Rawlinge, 8 September.
ffrancis, s. Richard Yeldam, 13 September.
Dorcas, d. John Reade, 14 September.
John, s. Henrie Smith, 13 November.
Dorcas, d. William Butcher, of Gensforde, 22 November.
Richard, s. William Butcher, aforesaid, 22 November.
ffrancis, s. Henrie Billirod, otherwise called Bust, 29 November.
Robert, s. Robert Smith, 27 December.
William, s. Hugh Rawlinge, 26 December.
Wa[l]ter, s. Christopher Taylor, 27 December.
Samuel, s. Robert Edward, 5 Januarie.
Alice, d. Richard Gipps, the last Januarie.

[6] Anne, d. William Earelope, otherwise called Connye, 21 March.

1574 ffrances, d. John Hamonte, 24 April.
William, s. John Clarke, 13 June.
Margarete, d. Edward Richardson, 23 Julie.
Margaret, d. William Boram, 8 August.
Leastrange, s. Henrie Snellocke, 22 August.
Margarete, d. Richard Eeverede, 29 August.
Marie, d. Thomas Bailye, 21 November.
William, s. John Harvie, 14 December.
Marie, d. the aforesaide John Harvie, 14 December.
Anna, d. Thomas Cracherood the elder, 19 Januarie.
Henrie, s. John Cirke, 13 Februarie.
Marie, d. Henrie Wayte, 20 Februarie.
William, s. Steven Cante, 20 March.

1575 John, s. Richard Hulle, 26 April.

William, s. Robert fflowere, 1 May.
Elizabeth, d. Thomas Browne, 3 May.
Barbara, d. William Redman, 15 May.
Susan, d. John Humfrie, 15 May.
Thomas, s. Thomas Aldrede, 19 June.
Robert, s. William Reade, 26 Julie.
Anne, d. Thomas Pollard, 4 September.
William, s. Christopher Fitch, 18 September.
William, s. William Bigge, 26 September.
Margarete, d. Henrie Gridlie, 31 December.
Susan, d. John Buttall, 26 Februarie.
Hugh, s. Hugh Rawlinge, 18 Februarie.
Priscilla, d. William Buttall, 4 March.

1576 Alyce, d. Edward Richardson, 9 Julie.
ffrances, d. William Butcher, 15 Julie.
William, s. William Reade, 7 August.
ffrancis, s. Henrie Fetforth, 12 August.
Winnefrede, d. Henrie Snellocke, 16 September.
Millicent, d. William Redman, 23 September.
Alyce, d. William Edward, 13 November.
R*   s. Richard Butcher, 19 Februarie.
Joane, d. John Bateman, 20 March.
Marie, d. Steven Cante, 20 March.

[7]
1577 Elizabeth, d. John Brine, 26 March.
William, s. Thomas Browne, 3 April.
ffrances, d. Robert Edward, 5 April.
William, s. Thomas Cracherood the younger, 28 Julie.
Alice, d. John Greene, 3 November.
———, s. Richard Bateman, 3 November.
Rose, d. Robert Perrye, 24 November.
———, d. John Buttall, 17 December.
John, s. Richard Evered, 22 December.

1578 Robert, s. John Clarke, 1 April.
Ralfe, s. John Humfrie, 6 April.
John, s. ——— Horklye, 18 May.
Thomas, s. Thomas Cracherood, 15 June.
William, s. William Pollard, 18 November.

---

*Rest of name erased.

William, s. William Reade, 23 Julie.
Ralfe, s. William Reade, 23 Julie.
1579 Anne, d. Steven Cante, the last day of May.
Dorcas, d. William Redman, 18 June.
Henry Bateman was baptized 20 June.
Marie, d. Robert Edward, 13 August.
Alice, d. John Greene, 6 September.
Trefyna, d. William Boram, 13 September.
Annie, d. Richard Evered, 18 October.
Anne, d. Thomas Browne, 25 October.
John, s. Henrie Gridley, 22 November.
Richarde, s. Robert Smith, 22 November.
Margarete, d. Richard Perrye, 26 November.
Sarah, d. Richard Edward, 17 Januarie.
Thomas, s. William Buttall, 17 Januarie.
Elizabeth, d. William Pollard, 17 Januarie.
Henrie, s. John Bateman, 24 Januarie.
Matthew, s. Thomas Cracherood the younger, 24 Februarie.
John, s. John Bottall [sic], 24 Februarie.
1580 Henrie, s. John Clarke, 26 March.
Samuel, s. William Bigge, 15 May.
William, s. John Hammond, 15 June.
Audre, d. Richard Bocher, 15 June.
William, s. Edward Richardson, the last day of Julie.
Margarete, d. Robert George, 7 August.
Margarete, d. Thomas Bateman, 13 November.
Margarete, d. Thomas Garner, 20 November.
Thomas, s. William Rede, 5 March.
1581 Robert, s. Henrie Snellocke, 8 May.
Anne, d. William Harrington, 14 May.
[8] Sarah, d. John Briant, 21 May.
Henrie, s. Thomas Baylie, 2 Julie.
Jane, d. Thomas Cracherood the elder, 16 Julie.
William, s. Robert Joley, 1 September.
William, s. Egidii Rede, 29 October.
Sarah, d. William Bacon, 26 November.
Anne, d. Thomas Cracherood the younger, 21 Januarie.
Marie, d. Richard Bateman, 28 Januarie.
John, s. Robert Perry, 12 Februarie.

1582 Judeth, d. Steven Cante, 25 March.
Elizabeth, d. Edward Richardson, 1 April.
Margerie, d. Clement Boram, 1 April.
Henrie, s. Henrie Gridley, 8 April.
Christian, d. Robert Edward, 17 April.
William, s. Robert Overed, 17 April.
Barbara, d. Richard Evered, 22 April.
William, s. Thomas Bateman, 20 May.
John, s. Thomas Browne, 20 May.
Anne, d. Thomas Garner, 24 June.
Robert, s. Robert George, 1 Julie.
Elizabeth, d. Robert Greene, 14 Julie.
William, s. John Bosall, 28 Julie.
James, s. John Harrington, yeoman, 11 August.
John, s. John Harrington, paup., 11 August.
Judith, d. William Pollard, 9 September.
Joane, d. John Waford, 13 October.
Anne, d. John Hamond, 4 November.
Margarete, d. William Bosall, 20 Januarie.
Alyce, d. Roger Edward, 3 Februarie.

1583 John, s. John Freer, 7 April.
Dorothy, d. Egidii Rede, 7 April.
Elizabeth, d. John Greene, 26 Maye.
Thomas, s. Edward Laver, 2 June.
Ishmael, s. Margarete Clarke, adult, 13 June.
James, s. John Harrington, 29 September.
William, s. William Bacon, 6 October.
Briget, d. John Bryant, 13 October.
William, s. Richard Bucher, 27 October.
Richard, s. Richard Evered, 10 November.
Elizabeth, d. William Reade, 10 December.
Elizabeth, d. Robert Perry, 15 December.
Anne, d. John Wafer, 22 December.
William, s. William Cracherood the younger, 25 December.
Thomas, s. Nicholas Garnet, 15 Januarie.

[9] Jane, d. Thomas Cracherood the younger, 23 Januarie.
Marie, d. Thomas Carey, 2 Februarie.
Elizabeth, d. Thomas Bateman, 1 March.
Edmund, s. John Hamond, 15 March.

1584 Joyce, d. John Hampton, 3 May.
Samuel, s. Robert Hamond, 24 May.
Robert, s. Robert Edward, 8 June.
Alyce, d. Thomas Garner, 9 August.
Margarete, d. William Harrington, 29 August.
Joyce, d. Richard* Bateman, 29 August.
Edward, s. John Reade, 20 September.
Steven, s. Steven Cante, 4 October.
Henrie, s. Egidii Reades, 1 November.
Edward, s. William Bigge, 15 November.
James, s. Edward Richard, 15 November.
Penelope, d. Richard Evered, 13 December.
Samuel, s. Robert Overed, 17 Januarie.
Joane, d. Henrie Gridley, 17 Januarie.
Thomas and Robert, s. John Harrington, paup., 31 Januarie.
Anne, d. Henrie Bateman, 1 March.

1585 Alyce, d. John Bosall, 12 April.
Alyce, d. Robert Perrye, 1 May.
Marie, d. John Harrington, 2 May.
Andrew, s. Roger Edward, 2 May.
William, s. John Teball, 9 May.
John, s. John Greene, 9 May.
——, s. John Waford, 16 May.
William, s. William Edward, jun., 20 June.
Barbara, d. Henrie Snellocke the younger, 11 Julie.
Thomas, s. Robert George, 18 Julie.
Anne, d. John Sewell, 26 September.   [ber.
Henrie, s. Elizabeth Chunke, widow [sic], 14 Novem-
Martha, born in fornication of Humfrye Elsworth and Anne Hewes, 15 Januarie.

1586 Sarah, d. Thomas Bateman, 4 April.
Dorcas, d. William Bigge, 7 April.
Leastrange, s. William Firmin, 7 April.
John, s. Thomas Cracherood, jun., 10 April.
Anne, d. William Buttall, 15 April [sic].
Nathan, s. Richard Bateman, jun., 1 May.
Marie, d. Lodovice Brett, 1 May.

---
*Henrie erased and Richard inserted.

Hester, d. Edward Tilbrok, 1 May.
John, s. John Bateman, 15 May.
Henrie, s. William Cracherood, 18 May.
Anne, d. John Briant, 23 May.
Daniel, s. William Home, 5 June.
[10] Margarete, d. Thomas Browne, 16 June.
Richard, s. Henrie Snellocke, 6 September.
Sarah, d. John Perrye, 2 October.
Ann, d. John Cob, 10 October.
Matthew, s. Henrie Bever, 4 December.
Josias, s. John Pollard, 5 December.
ffaith, d. Richard Bocher, 11 December.
John, s. John Read, 26 Februarie.
Robert, s. James Robinson, 12 March.
———, of Robert Linwood, 12 March.
1587 William, s. Clement Boram, 9 April.
Thomas, s. John Waford, 14 May.
William, s. William Linsye, 23 May.
———, William Ferrer, 23 May.
Henrie, s. John Reade, jun., 11 June.
Anne, d. Henrie Snellock, jun., 30 Julie.
John, s. ——— Sache, 14 August.
Sarah, d. Steven Cante, 10 September.
John, s. John Hamond, 17 September.
Richard, s. Henrie Gridley, 24 September.
Richard, s. John Gipps, 24 September.
Brigitte, d. Thomas Cracherood, jun., 1 October.
Tamesine, d. William Cracherood, 1 October.
Jone, d. William Browne, 1 October.
Elizabeth, d. William Edward, 19 November.
Clemens Tyboll, 19 November.
Rose, d. Edward Richardson, 3 Januarie.
Richard Howborowe, 3 Januarie.
ffrancis, s. John Somes, 4 Februarie.
Elizabeth, d. Richard Bateman, jun., 18 Februarie.
1588 Sarah, d. William Edward, of Bradfield, 25 Julie.
Margarie, d. Edward Osteler, 25 August.
Helene, d. Robert Tiler, 21 September.
Daniel, s. Robert Perrye, 29 September.
Thomas, s. Roger Edward, 13 October.

Susan, d. Henrie Snellocke, jun., 27 October.
Mattew, s. —— Brette, 11 November.
Rebekah, d. John Bryant, 11 November.
Anne, d. John Hart, 2 Februarie.
John, s. John Pollard, 9 Februarie.
Henrie, s. Richard Overed, 2 March.
Elizabeth, d. James Russell, 9 March.
1589 Anne, d. William ffirmin, 22 April.
Anne, d. Richard ——, 1 May.
[11] John Mariver, 25 Maye.
Alice ffyche, 25 May.
Elizabeth, d. John Reade, 29 June.
Ralfe, s. William Boram, 6 Julie.
John, s. Thomas Harvie, 27 Julie.
Prudence, d. John Cosin, 10 August.
John, s. John Warman, 14 September.
Alice, d. William Linsye, 14 September.
Hellena, d. Edward Osteler, 21 September.
Humfrie, s. Thomas Cracherood, jun., 25 September.
Marie, d. William Cracherood, 29 September.
Henrie, s. Henrie Snellock, jun., 5 October.
Thomas, s Thomas Corke, 5 October.
Susan, d. John Bird, 26 October.
Elizabeth, d. John Gipps, 9 November.
Susan, d. Jo— Ray de Gosfield,* 11 November.
Susan, d. Robert Tiler, 21 December.
William, s. William Thorogood, 18 Januarie.
Cicely, d. Robert Some, 18 Januarie.
Susan, d. Richard Bocher, 1 Februarie.
John, s. Marie Tilbroke, widow, 2 Februarie.
Grace, d. Steven Cante, 16 Februarie.
Elizabeth, d. William Ferrer, 16 Februarie.
Marie, d. Thomas Garner, 1 March.
Marie, d. Anne Bocher, borne in fornication, 1 March.
Elizabeth Howborowe, 1 March.
1590 Jane, d. Nicholas Reade, 5 May.
Elizabeth, d. William Edwards de Bradfields, 9 June.
William, s. Henrie Gridley, 28 Julie.

---

*Gosfield is a neighboring village.

William, s. Thomas ffyche.
Orphane, s. —— Powle, 11 October.
Christopher, s. Henrie Snellocke, jun., 24 November.
Henrie, s. Davide Marner, 29 November.
Anne, d. John Cosin, 6 December.
Margarete, d. William Argent, 1 Januarie.
John, s. Lewis Brett, 9 Februarie.
Roda, d. William Thorogood, 15 Februarie.
Susan, d. William Edward, jun., 25 Februarie.
Mercie, d. John Pollard, last day of Februarie.

1591 Susan, d. Thomas Bateman, 28 March.
Thomas. s. Richard Evered, 18 April.
William, s. William Bust, 2 May.
Joane, d. Henrie Edward, 9 May.
Rose, d. Henrie Laver, 9 May.
Robert, s. Thomas Cracherood, jun., 16 May.
Susan, d. John Bryant, 16 May.
Edward, s. William Cracherood, 20 June.
Zacharias, s. —— Marner, 15 August.
Thomas, s. Thomas Plomb, 15 August.

[12] Alice, d. Edward Osteler, 12 September.
Sarah, d. Henrie Bret, 28 September.
Thomas, s. Thomas Harvie, 10 October.
Richard, s. Isaac Hart, 28 November.
Rose, d. Henrie Snellocke, 19 December.
Grissell, d. Robert Tiler, 9 Januarie.
Edward, s. Thomas Somes, 5 March.
Tamasin, d. John Gipps, 12 March.
Matthew and Katherine, chn. William Thorogood, 23 March.

1592 William, s. William Browne, 9 April.
Sarah, d. Thomas Edward, 4 June.
Rebekah, d. Nicholas Reade, 4 June.
Anne, d. Robert Rolfe, 18 June.
John, s. John Cosin, 18 June.
Henrie, s. John Reade, 25 June.
Edwards, s. Steven Cante, 20 August.
Thamesin, d. James Russell, 17 September.
Matthew, s. John Hamond, 1 October.
Thomas, s. Thomas Plomb, 29 October.

Anne, d. William Cosin, 29 October.
Ezichiel, s. Izhak Cornwell, 5 November.
Margaret, d. Thomas Lamson, 1 Januarie.
Henrie, s. Lewis Brette, 14 Januarie.
William, s. John Humfrye, 28 Januarie.
Elizabeth, d. —— Browne, 5 Februarie.
Matthew, s. Henrie Snellocke, 27 Februarie.
William, s. Richard Payne, 3 March.

1593 William, s. Edward Osteler, 1 April.
Susan and Margaret, ds. William Edward, 1 May.
John, s. William Bocher, 7 June.
Joane, d. Thomas Cracherood, 8 Julie.
ffrances, d. William Thorogood, 22 Julie.
Sarah, d. Robert Tyler, 25 Julie.
——, of John Reade, 23 September.
William, s. William ffirmin, 27 September.
William, s. Henrie Pettit, 21 October.
John, s. John Bryant, 4 November.
Matthew, s. Thomas Hurrell, 9 September.
Anne, d. Thomas Tonge, 6 Januarie.
Robert, s. Robert Marner, 10 Februarie.

[13] Susan, d. Richard Bateman, 17 Februarie.
1594 Robert, s. Robert Hogg, 21 April.
Joane, d. Lewis Turner, 12 May.
Winifrede, d. James Russell, 19 May.
Elizabeth, d. Lewis Brett, 26 May.
John, s. Robert Rolfe, 9 June.
Marie, d. Matthew Whiting, 18 Julie.
George, s. John Gipps, 28 Julie.
Margarete, d. Henrie Brette, 28 Julie.
ffrances, d. William Greene, 25 August.
Dorcas, d. William Cracherood, 2 October.
Joseph, s. Izhak Cornwell, 6 October.
William, s. Jeremie Turkill, 6 October.
Thomas, s. William Browne, 17 November.
Elizabeth, d. Thomas Horkley, 25 November.
William, s. Davide Marner, 5 Januarie.
Winifrede, d. James Russell, 28 Januarie.
John, s. John Clarke, 4 Februarie.
John, s. Edward Osteler, 2 March.

REGISTER. — BAPTISMS. 17

Elizabeth, d. Thomas Harvie, 20 March.
1595 Alyce, d. "of a certeine begger", 30 March.
Samuel, s. William Edward, 6 April.
Thomas, s. Thomas Marner, 25 Maye.
John, s. Simon Greene, 6 Julie.
Robert, s. Robert Edward, 9 Julie.
Thomas, s. John Pollard, 3 August.
————, of Brette, 10 August.
Elizabeth, of Robert Rolfe, 24 August.
Grace, d. Henry Snellock, 7 September.
William, s. William ffirmin, 7 September.
Alyce, d. John Amyce, 7 September.
Margarie, d. William Cracherood, 7 September.
John, s. John Playle, 13 November.
John, s. John Parker, 7 March.
1596 Thomas, s. Henry Pettitt, 25 March.
Sarah, d. Robert Tiler, 19 April.
————, of James Russell, 20 May.
Samuel, s. Robert Rolfe, 5 September.
Christopher, s. Christopher Snellock, 14 September.
William, s. William Edward of Bradfields, 7 November.
Hester, d. Richard Bateman, 13 November.
[14] John, s. John ffisher, 5 December.
Alce, d. William ffisher, 6 Januarie.
Torearie, d. Henrie Snellock, 16 Januarie.
John, s. John ffiche, 30 Januarie.
William, s. William Greene, 20 Februarie.
Thomas, s. Jonah Spiltimber, 20 Februarie.
Susan, d. Robert Hogg, 24 Februarie.
Sarah, d. Zacharie Smyth, 5 March.
1597 Joseph, s. ———— Bragge, 10 April.
Samuel, s. Edward Osteler, 17 April.
Anne, d. William Bocher, 8 May.
Rachel, d. John Gipps, 8 May.
Robert, s. Thomas Edward, 12 September.
Timothye, s. ———— Cob, 21 September.
Elizabeth, d. Richard Edward, 14 October.
Susan, d. William Birde, 17 November.
Thomas, s. John Platte, 19 November.
John, s. John ffisher, 20 Februarie.

Susan, d. Edmund Whiting, 20 Februarie.
Elizabeth, d. Thomas Plombe, 20 March.
1598 Anne, d. Richard Payne, 2 April.
William, s. Simon Greene, 23 April.
Helena, d. of Habel Laver, 30 April.
Emily, d. of Thomas Harvie, 24 May.
Dorothy, d. John Pollard, 28 May.
Susan, d. Richard Wilson, 27 August.
Robert, s. Robert Tiler, 28 August.
Margarete, d. John ffiche, 17 September.
William, s. William Greene, butcher, 1 October.
John, s. Robert Warner, 9 October.
William, s. William Bocher of Gensforde, 15 October.
Elizabeth, d. Edmund Bryant, 15 October.
Elizabeth, d. Henrie Pettit, 30 October.
Joane, d. Robert Rolfe, 24 December.
William, s. Richard Edward, 24 December.
1599 John, s. John Redgewell, 9 Aprill.
Steven, s. Christopher Reade, 25 April.
Dorcas, d. Henry Laver, 26 April.
William, s. John Clarke, 29 April.
Thomas, s. John Humfrye, 1 May.
Marie, d. Robert Hogge, 1 May.
Stephanus Reade.*
David, s. David Warner, 17 May.
Mary, d. John Fisher, 27 May.
Susanna, d. Edward Ostler, 27 May.
William, s. John Lawson, 7 August.
Richard, s. Richard Titirel, 14 August.
Robert, s. —— Sibley, 30 September.
William, s. William Butcher, alias Adams, 3 June.
Barbara, d. John Fimis, 11 February.

---

*A line is drawn through this name. The record is apparently a copy in the same hand to here, and this may be the signature of the copyist. The same hand apparently makes the next 11 entries, but there are irregularities unobservable before, and the ink is very bad, and faded. The ink becomes good, and the handwriting entirely changes its character, and becomes larger with the entry Thomas Greene, but changes back again with Margaret Pettitt (1 Nov. 1600). From that point forwards the changes in ink and handwriting are frequent, the different number of entries on a folio will give some idea of the variation in the size of the characters.

REGISTER. — BAPTISMS. 19

        Mary, d. Jonas Spiltimber, 20 February.
        Margery, d. Robert Tongue, 11 February.
        Elizabeth, d. Thomas Chamberlain, 25 February.
        Thomas, s. William Greene, 18 Februarie.
1600 Richard, s. William Greene, 30 March.
        John, s. William Battie, 30 March.
        Susanna, d. Gabriell Grante, 6 April.
        Rachell, d. Abell Laver, 6 April.
        Henry, s. Thomas Harvie, 20 April.
        Thomasin, d. William Edward, 30 May.
        Daniell, s. William Butcher, 30 May.
        Sara, d. William Edward, jun., 17 August.
        Winifrede, d. John Hayle, 31 August.
        Rose, d. Richard Edward, 8 Septembe [sic].
        Sara, d. Thomas Gow, 28 Septembe.
        Hercules, s. widow ffisher, 28 Septembe.
        Mary, d. Thomas Warner, 26 Octobe.
        Thomazine, d. —— Chamberlin, 26 Octobe.
[15]   Margaret, d. George Lane, 9 Novembe.
        Mary, d. John Constable, 16 November.
        Elizabeth, d. Richard Payne, 16 Novembe.
        John, s. John Baylie, 23 Novembe.
        Mary, d. John Ridgewell, 30 Novembe.
1601 Catheren, d. John Eoull, 1 November.
        John, s. John Gipp, 1 November.
        Margaret, d. William [erased] Pettitt, 1 November.
        Thomas, s. Henry Cirke, 22 November.
1601 Henry, s. Henry Lande, 6 January.
1601 Mary, d. Richard Titrell, 6 January.
1601 Thomas, s. Thomas Sybley, 9 ffebruary.
1601 Agnes, d. William Butcher, 23 ffebruary.
1601 Robert, s. William Butcher, 7 March.
1602 Elizabeth, d. William Grene, 30 May.
1602 William, s. Mr. Robert Rolfe, 1 June.
        Margaret, d. Adler Newman, 27 June [sic].
        ffrancis, d. Michael Clerk, 8 August.
        Robert, s. John Pollard, 8 August.
        ——, d. Richard Edwarde, 8 August.
        Dorothy, d. Robt. Hoy, 6 September.
        Peter, s. Davy Warner, 7 October.

William, s. William Battie, 7 October.
Edwards, s. Nicholas Evens, 7 October.
Agnes, d. Thomas Harvey, 19 October.
Alyce, d. Robert Spiltimber, 7 November.
Robert, s. Robert Clarke, 18 [?] November.
Ann, d. John Ridgewell, 23 January.
William, s. Thomas Plumb, 30 January.
Cicely, d. Edmund Briant, 9 ffebruary.
John, s. Samuel Edwarde, 8 March.

Jacobi primo.
1603 Mary, d. John Bayley, 5 May.
Ann, d. Robert Edwarde, 21 June.
Margaret, d. John Amis, 21 June.
Margery, d. John Start, 3 July.
Edwards, s. John Pitches, 17 July.
John, s. Richard Edward, 11 September.
ffrancis, s. Christopher Read, 14 September.
John, s. John Pettitt, 18 September.
Susan, d. John Pettitt, 18 September.
Mary, d. Richard Payne, 5 November.
Alyce, d. Richard Tittrell, 15 January.
Lucy, d. Thomas Sibble, 5 March.
Ann, d. William Butcher, 18 March.

Jacobi 2.
1604 John, s. Edmund Bryant, 20 April.
William, s. William Horner, 20 April.
John, s. John Perry, 22 May.
Ales, d. Adlan [*sic*] Newman, 9 Sept.
John, s. Richard Edwarde, 12 Sept.
Samuel, s. John Parker, 11 October.
Robert, s. Robert Spiltimber, 14 October.
Peter, s. Thomas Harvy, 28 October.
[16] Marian, d. Saunder Bulloynes, 11 November.
Henry, s. Atlas Evans, 11 November.
Susan, d. John Ridgwell, 18 November.
Priscilla, d. Michael Clerke, 13 January.
Dorathy, d. Thomas Warner, 20 January.
John, s. Henry Lawer, 7 ffebruary.
Ales, d. William Batte, 7 ffebruary.
William, s. John Gips, 6 March.

REGISTER. — BAPTISMS.

Jacobi 3.
1605 Mathews, s. Robert Edwarde, of ffullers, 25 March.
———, Thomas Plumbe, 7 Aprill.
Sara, d. James Shed, 5 May.
Sara, d. Thomas Chattowton, 19 May.
Henry, s. John Smith, 26 May.
Anne, d. William Greene, 13 June.
John, s. William Waford, 31 July.
Robert, s. Richard Edward, 29 August.
John, s. William Seman, 22 December.
Ann, d. John Amis, 26 December.
Robert, s. Edmund Briant, 1 January.
Richer, s. Ales Hart, 13 January.
William, s. Thomas Sibble, 4 February.

Jacobi quarto.
1606 John, s. John Fox, 30 March.
William, s. Thomas Chatterton, 1 June.
Jonathan, s. Robert Deborax, 2 June.
Ales, d. Richard Batte, 16 June.
Ann, d. John Start, 24 June.
Robert, s. Thomas Mathew, 29 June.
Clemens, s. Clemens Borham, 20 June.
Richard, s. "Mr. Richard King, parson of this towne," 27 June.
ffrancis, s. John Brown webster, 23 July.
Dorothy, d. Richard Edward, 30 September.
Sara, d. Thomas Harvy, 7 October.
Robert, s. John Perry, 12 Octobe.
Ann, d. Alexander Bulloyne, 12 October.
John, s. Robert Hogge, 2 November.
Thomas, s. Thomas Browne, 5 December.
Alexander, s. Thomas Plumbe, 21 December.
Mary, d. John Smith, 17 Januarie.
Sara, d. Robert Edward, 20 Januarie.
William, s. William Waford, 5 February.
Alice, d. John Ridgewell, February.
Robert, s. Hercules Newman, 1 March.
Margaret, d. Hercules Evans, 20 March.

1607 William, s. James Sheade, 6 Aprill.
Richard, s. Richard Payne, 22 Aprill.

Sara, d. John Langton, 4 July.
Thomas, s. Henry Laver, 18 Julie.
Elizabeth, d. Richard Titterill, 2 August.
Mary, d. John Brande, 15 Sept.
Ann, d. William Punnell, 31 Jan.
Thomas, s. Clemens Borham, 18 Feb.
Mary, d. Mr. Richard Kinge, parson, 21 Feb.
Dorothy, d. William Butcher, 28 Feb.
An, d. Thomas Gardiner, 3 March.

1608 John, s. Thomas Plumme, 20 June.
Henry, s. John Gips, 26 June.
Elizabeth, d. Jeremye Payman, 2 July.
Margaret, d. Robert Edwardes, Fullers, 28 July.
Margaret, d. William Waford, 10 August.

[17] Nathaniel, s. John Starte, 16 August.
John, s. Christopher Reade, 4 October.
Alice, d. William Bateman, 11 October.
John, s. Richarde Raven, 9 Nov.
Barbara, d. William Battye, 20 Dec.
Simon, s. John Foxe, 17 Jan.
Thomas, s. Thomas Gardiner, 11 Feb.
Francis, d. John Perry, 26 Feb.

1609 Nathaniel, s. Briget Brian, begotten in fornication, 17 April.
Thomas, s. Robert Devorax, 19 Aprill.
Richard, s. Hercules Evins, 14 May.
John, s. Jerome Perman, 10 October.
Michael, s. Michael Richardson, 19 October.
John, s. Mr. John Cracherood, 24 October.
William, s. Robert Pollard, 28 October.
James, s. James Shedd, 24 October.
William, s. Robert George, 11 January.
Thomas, s. Thomas Plumbe, of Olivers, 12 March.
Edward, s. John Start, 23 March.

1610 Alice, d. Robert Clerke, 29 March.
Elizabeth, d. Adlan Newman, 1 Aprill.
Richard, s. Richard Raven, 1 April.
William, s. Andrew Edward, 7 April.
Rose, d. John Drury, 7 April.
William, s. John Redgwell, 7 April.

Thomas, s. Robert Edward, of the fermen, 8 July.
Dorothy, d. Thomas Browne, 7 July.
Joane, d. Richard ffinch, 22 July.
[18] Judeth, d. William Horne, 10 August.
Margaret, d. William Dunnell, 12 August.
John, s. Richard Titterill, 12 August.
Ann, d. Robert Edward, of fullers, 22 August.
Ann, d. Clement Boram, 9 Sept.
Dorothy, d. William Bateman, 13 September.
Ann, d. Daniell Butcher, 11 November.
Thomas, s. John Perry, 2 December.
ffrancis, d. John Smith, 4 December.
Ann, d. Richard Butcher, 20 December.
Ellin, d. Robert Pollard, 13 January.
1611 John, s. John Hawksbee, 24 Aprill.
Johanna, d. Robert Denovan, 13 May.
Catheren, d. Robert Edward, jun., 21 May.
William, s. Atlas Evans, 23 May.
Thomas, s. William Battie, 30 May.
Daniell, s. Michael Richardson, 27 June.
William, s. Thomas Gardiner, 13 July.
Elizabeth, d. Thomas Plumb, 29 August.
Margaret, d. Richard Kinge, Doctor in Divinity, 19 September.
Ann, d. Thomas Browne, 3 October.
Thomas, s. Thomas Mathew, 18 November.
Marye, d. Christopher Roote, 21 January.
Richard, s. John Start, 28 January.
Margaret, d. John Quie, 25 February.
Elizabeth, d. Richard Edward, 27 February, 1616.
Sara, d. Henry Pettit, jun., 28 February.
Mary, d. William Overed, 18 March.
Sara, d. Robert Hogge, 23 March.
1612 Margaret, d. James Shedd, 4 Aprill.
Elizabeth, d. Robert Harrington, 14 Aprill.
Alice, d. Edward Clay, 11 May.
Elizabeth, ———, ———.
Margaret, d. Laurence More, 12 June.
John, s. Thomas Balie, 2 Julie.
William, s. Clement Boreham, 28 Julie.

Elizabeth, d. Jerome Perman, 30 Julie.
Dorcas, d. John Cracherood, gentleman, 6 August.
Georg, s. William Waford, 3 Sept.
William, s. William Bateman, 22 Sept.
Mary, d. Philip Ansell, 23 Sept.
Joseph, s. Michael Richardson, 14 October.
Elizabeth, d. Henrie Evans, 14 October.
Sara, d. Robert Pollard, 19 November.
Elizabeth, d. Thomas Gipp, 19 October.
Marie, d. Samuell Bateman, 13 January.
William, s. Richard Raven, 21 January.
John, s. Robt. Edwards, 7 Febr.
William, s. John Perry.

1613 Eliza, d. William Sparke, 25 March.
Susan, d. William Batty, 27 April.
Henery, s. William Smith, 23 May.
Robt., s. John Browne, 30 May.
Samuel, s. Andrew Edwards, 20 June.
Joanna, d. John Start, 28 July.
Annie, d. —— Medcalfe, 2 Aug.

[18] Mary, d. Robert Edwards, jun., [date illegible].
Sept. 30. Benjamin, s. Thomas Bateman.
October 3. Hellen, d. Samuel Dod.
November 5. Susan, d. William Overhead.
Decemb. 12. William, s. Edward Brown.
Jan. 6. Mary, d. Richard Kendhel.
Jan. 13. Samuell, s. Samuell Bateman.
Feb. 19. William, s. Robert Edwards the greater.
March 17. Susan, d. Mr. Richard Kinge, Dr. of Divinity.

1614 April 10. Susan, d. William Levit.
April 21. Mary, d. William Bacon.
April 26. Mary, d. Nathaniell Bateman.
June 2. Susan, d. Richard Harrington.
July 17. Laurance, s. Laurance Moore.
Sept. 18. William, s. Richard Butcher.
Sept. 1. Robert, s. Thomas Buttall.
Sept. 27. Mathew, s. William Butcher.
Octob. 2. John, s. Michaell Richardson.
Oct. 28. Josias, s. Josias Pollard.

Oct. 28. Alice, d. Robert Pollard.
Nov. 18. John, s. Nichelaus Evens.
Nov. 22. Jonathan, s. Christopher Roote.
Jan. 7. Edward, the base sonne of Elizabeth Grene.
Jan. 12. John, s. John Quie.
Jan. 19. Daniel, s. Richard Raven.
Jan. 31. Alice, d. William Sparke.
Feb. 2. Anne, d. Edward Clay.
Feb. 12. Stephen, s. Clement Boreham.
Feb. 21. John, s. William Edwards.
March 11. Ede, base daughter Adwy Fisher.
March 18. Thomas, s. William Bateman.
March 19. Daniell, s. Henry Bayley.

1615
May 4. Anne, d. William Smith.
May 2. William, s. Robert Medcalfe.
June 6. Hennery, s. Hennery Pettitt.
June 11. Ellen, d. Jeames Shedd.
Julie 21. John, s. John Dod.
June 27. Elizabeth, d. Robert Warner, jun.
Sep. 24. Robert, s. Thomas Butcher.
Nov. 2. Elizabeth, d. John Start.
Nov. 19. Nicholas, s. Nicholas Smith.
Decem. 2. Mary, d. John Perry.
Jan. 11. Barbery, d. John Pollard.
Jan. 21. Alice, d. Edward Moore.
Jan. 21. Daniel, s. Hennery Smith.
Jan. 28. Nathan, s. Nathan Bateman.
Jan. 30. William, s. William Cooper.
Decem. 21. Thomas, s. George Hogg.
Feb. 1. Sarah, d. Josias Pollard.
March 1. Martha, d. Jeremie Perman.
March 12. Jeames, s. Richard Kendall.
March 14. Elizabeth, d. Richard Harrington.

1616
April 2. Anne, d. William Sparke.
Rebecca, d. Daniel Dod.
May 21. Elizabeth, d. Robert Edwardes, jun.
June 2. Robert, s. Richard Titterill.
June 16. Rose, d. William Cooke.
June 24. Judith, d. Richard King.

Aug. 4. Susan, d. Thomas Gardner.
Aug. 13. Ellenor, d. Mr. John Cracherood.
Aug. 25. William, s. William Read.
Aug. 27. Robertah, d. Christopher Roote.
Sept. 1. Margaret, d. William Horne.
Novem. 24. Thomas, s. Thomas Brewer.
Decem. 1. Elizabeth, d. Giles Elsing.
Decem. 8. Robert, s. Robert Pollard.
Jan. 12. John, s. Robert Medcalf.
Jan. 19. Anne, d. John Drury.
Jan. 19. Susanna, d. Richard Gipps.
Jan. 23. William, s. William Bacon.
Feb. 26. Anne, d. Arthur Winterfloud.
Feb. 28. Elizabeth, d. Mihil[?] Osborne.
March 2. John, s. Richard Butcher.
March 4. Margaret, d. William Butcher.
March 19. William, s. William Levite.
March 19. Thomas & Alse, s. & d. Richard Raven.

1617 March 27. Susan, d. Henry Harrington.
April 8. Mary, d. Milvill Richardson.
April 21. Barbara, d. Robert Warner.
April 21. Lettice, d. John Start.
April 22. Edmund, s. Jeremie Parmeter.
May 22. Susauna, d. William Bateman.
June 15. Margaret, d. Thomas Robinson.
June 19. John, s. Thomas Dwe[?] alias Mathew.
Oct. 3. John Smithson, s. John Smithson.
Oct. 19. William, s. Edward Clay.
Oct. 23. Ric^d Wight, s. Thomas Wight.
Nov. 9. Nicholas, s. —— Traylor.
Nov. 29. Emma, d. James Qui.
Dec. 4. Anne, d. William Edwards, Bradfields.
Dec. 10. William, s. Moyses Wallis.
Jan. 16. William, s. Henry Bayley.
Jan. 22. Elizabeth, d. Nathan Barman.
Jan. 25. Henry, s. John Dod.
Feb. 16. William, s. Daniell Dod.
March 1. Dennes, s. Giles Elsing.

1618 April 6. Sara, d. William Bard.
April 8. Susan, d. Thomas Trapner.

Mai 4. Susan, d. Richard Kendall.
[20] Mai 27. Henry, s. Samuel Smith.
June 15. Richard, s. Samuel Simons, gent.
June 28. Thomas, s. Richard Rane.
June 29. Joseph, s. Joseph Mariner.
June 30. John, s. Nicholas Smith.
July 2. William, s. William Smith.
Aug. 2. Mary, d. James Shed.
Sept. 17. Robert, s. Robert Edwards.
Sept. 29. ffelix, s. ffelix Torinne.
Oct. 1. Mary, d. John Pollard.
Oct. 4. *William, s. Thomas Brewer.
Oct. 8. Mary, d. George Hogg.
Nov. 1. Joseph, s. John Simpson.
Nov. 10. Henry, s. Henry Petitt.
Nov. 19. Anne, d. Thomas Andrews.
Nov. 27. Thomas, s. John Start.
Jan. 6. Grisill, d. William Levett.
Jan. 14. Elizabeth, d. Jeremie Parmeter.
Jan. 27. Daniel, s. Michael Richardsonne.
Jan. 31. Henrie, s. Henrie Baylie.
Feb. 7. Henrie, s. William Read.
Feb. 9. Margarett, d. Robert Warner.
Feb. 19. Grace, d. William Cooke.
1619 March 29. Avis, d. William ffitch and Crissie his wife was baptized.
April 20. John, s. Robert Pollard & Ellen.
April 8. Richard, s. Thomas Wight & Edith.
April 17. Dorcas, d. Moses Wallis & Elizabeth.
April 25. Margaret, d. Clement Borham & Luce.
April 27. ffrances, d. Samuell Edwards, jun., & ffrances.
May 20. Elizabeth, d. Richard King & Margarett.
June 10. Mary, d. William Sparke & Catherine.
June 13. John, s. Michell Osburne & Marie.
July 7. William, s. Thomas Mathew & Margerie.
July 15. Anne, d. Laurence More & Elizabeth.
Aug. 15. Alice, d. Richard Butcher.
Oct. 3. Robert, s. Nathaniell Horne & Judith.
Novem. 9. Dorothy, d. Samuel Simons & Dorothe.

Novem. 18. Sara, d. William Bateman & ffrances [?]
Oct. 9. Anne, d. William Butcher, of Gainsford, & Margaret.
Decem. 17. Marie, d. Roger Hoyden & Sara.
[21] Decem. 20. Marie, d. Ambrose Tompson & Tomasyn.
Jan. 6. Joane, d. John Drury & Ester.
Jan. 13. Thomas, s. Josias Pollard & Sara.
March 7. Margaret, d. Thomas Trapnell & Anne.
1620 April 2. Robert, s. William Read & Alice.
April 8. Samuell, s. Samuell Hammond and Anne.
April 19. Thomas, s. John Allston & Anne.
April 20. Henry, s. Nathan Bateman & Mary.
April 20. George, s. Joseph Mariner & Mary.
April 26. Martha, d. William Edwards, de Bradfields, & Ane.
May 9. Elizabeth, d. Robert Trilne & Amis.
May 15. Frances, d. Clement Boreham & Luce.
May 22. Richard, s. Richard Edwards.
May 25. William, s. William Briant & Elizabeth.
June 3. Sarah, d. Richard Larke & Esther.
June 6. John, s. William Smith & Anne.
June 29. John, s. John Pollard & Elizabeth.
July 2. Thomas, s. Thomas Robinson & Margaret.
July 2. Anne, d. John ffisher & Bridgett.
July 6. John, s. George Hogge & Elizabeth.
July 6. Nathan, s. Richard Rane & Alse.
Aug. 5. William, s. William Sparke & Catherine.
Aug. 20. Henry, s. Robert Laver & Mary.
Sept. 19. Margaret, d. Edward Clay & Anne.
Sept. 19. Tomazine, d. ffelix Torrine & Mary.
Nov. 21. Elizabeth, d. Samuel Edwards & ffrances.
Dec. 17. Margaret, d. William Bacon & Marye.
Dec. 18. William, s. John Quie and Sara.
Jan. 5. Tomazin, base daughter of John Clarke & Elizabeth Browne.
Feb. 1. Esthamoth, s. Milvill Richards.
Feb. 10. John, s. Thomas Gardiner & Sara.
March 18. Elizabeth, d. Henry Petit & Sara.
[22]
1621 April 5. Elizabeth, d. Robert Warner & Elizabeth.

April 29. Jane, d. Samuel Simons & Dorothee.
William, s. William ffitche & Grizell, 17 June.
Martha, d. Robert Edwards, the younger, & Catherin, 21 June.
Thomas, s. Thomas Hawkins & Anne, 1 July.
Susan, d. Ralph Sewell & Mary, 29 July.
Susan, d. James Shed & Mary, 29 July.
Richard, s. Samuell Hamond & Anne, 9 August.
Margaret, d. John Simpson & Elizabeth, 17 Sept.
William, s. Richard Edwards & Mary, 10 October.
Mary, d. Jerome Parmenter & Ann, 19 August.
Peter, s. Robert Pollard & Ellenor, 27 October.
Joseph, s. William Butcher & Margarett, 15 November.
Thomasin, d. Henry Bayly & Judith, 2 December.
Thomas, s. Thomas Trapnell & Anne, 10 Dec.
Joseph, s. Mary Tilbroke, 20 January.
Marie, d. William Pamplin & Sarah, 3 March.
John, s. Roger Hoyden & Sarah, 5 March.
Allice, d. Giles Elsing & Elizabeth, 24 March.

[23]
1622 John, s. John Start & Allice, 26 March.
Thomas, s. William Bryant & Elizabeth, 31 March.
Robert, s. John Pollard & Elizabeth, 31 March.
Dorcas, d. Thomas Cratcherode, gent., & Susan, 18 Aprill.
Anne, d. Samuel Simons, gent., & Dorothy, 25 April.
Sarah, d. John ffisher and Brigett, 28 April.
Thomasin, d. Jeremy Pearmaine & Thomasin, 5 May.
Robert, s. William Levett & Susan, 20 June.
Samuel, s. John Dod & Mary, 8 July.
Elizabeth, d. Richard Kendall & Anna, 5 Sept.
Thomas, s. Henry Paine & Mary, 15 Sept.
William, s. Joseph Marriner & Mary, 18 Sept.
William, s. Thomas Buttoll & Elizabeth, 22 Sept.
John, s. John Drury & Hester, 5 December.
John, s. William Read & Allice, 15 December.
Samuel, s. Nathaniel Horne & Joane, 12 January.
Robert, s. Robt. Traylor & Avis, 16 January.
[24] Margarett, d. Samuell Hamond & Anne, 23 January.
Ellen, d. Clement Borum & Luce, 10 ffebruary.

Samuell, s. Richard Edwards & Mary, 9 March.
1623 Susan, d. Michael Richardson & Elizabeth, 1 April.
Mary, d. John Read & Mary, 15 Aprill.
Joane, d. Rafe Sewell & Mary, 2 June.
Susan, d. Henry Pettitt & Sarah, 20 June.
Margarett, d. Laurence More & Elizabeth, 10 August.
John, s. Thomas Cratcherode & Susan, 13 August.
Robert, s. Robert Warner & Elizabeth, 14 August.
Tomasin, d. Theodore Cole & Tomasin, 26 August.
Mary, d. Robert Wentford & Anna, 28 August.
William, s. William Edwards & Anne, 9 October.
Samuell, s. Samuell Symons & Dorothy, 29 October.
Jane, d. William Pamplin & Sarah, 14 December.
Richard, s. Robert Pollard & Ellenor, 1 February.
Mary, d. Barnard Sibly & ffrancis, 10 ffebruary.
Arnold, s. Arnold Wade & Mary, 12 ffebruary.
[25] Sarah, d. Thomas Hale & Susan, 25 ffebruary.
1624 Anne, d. John Mising & Anne, 2 May.
John, s. Robert Edwards & Katherin, 6 May.
John, s. William ffitch & Grizell, 13 June.
Elizabeth, d. John Gardiner, gent., & Jane, 15 July.
William, s. John Simpson & Elizabeth, 25 July.
Thomas, s. John Simpson & Elizabeth, 25 July.
Susan, d. John Quy & Sarah, 1 August.
Samuell, s. William Bryant & Elizabeth, 29 August.
Thomas, s. William Bacon & Mary, 28 September.
ffrancis, d. Edward Clay & Anne, 28 October.
Margarett, d. Richard Kendall & Anne, 16 November.
Grace, d. John Pollard & Elizabeth, 28 November.
Elizabeth, d. John Drury & Hester, 28 November.
Susan, d. Thomas Paynell & Grace, 2 Dec.
Henry, s. Henry Paine & Mary, 12 December.
Mary, d. Thomas Robinson, alias Butcher, & Margarett, 12 December.
Anne, d. Thomas Trapnell & Anne, 19 December.
Thomas, s. Richard Edwards & Mary, 19 December.
Elizabeth, d. Samuell Symons & Dorothy, 22 December.
[26] Susan, d. John Read & Mary, 3 January.
William, s. Roger Hoyden & Sarah, 11 January.

Theodore, s. Theodore Cole & Tamesin, 31 January.
Mary, d. Robert Warner & Elizabeth, 17 ffebruary.
Anne, d. Samuell Hamond & Anne, 17 March.
Susan, d. Richard Gyps & Susan, 20 March.
William, s. William Spark & Katherin, 21 March.

1625 Anne, d. Henrie Pettitt & Sarah, 28 Aprill.
Sarah, d. William Hart & Ellenor, 12 May.
Mary, d. Rafe Sewell & Mary, 17 May.
Agnes, d. Robert Wankford & Agnes, 4 July.
Elizabeth, d. John Warner & Elizabeth, 7 July.
George, s. George Gyps & Rebeckah, 10 July.
Thomas, s. Thomas Warner, the younger, & Dorothy, 28 July.
Sarah, d. William Read & Allice, 19 August.
Mary, d. Thomas Greene & Mary, 8 Sept.
Susan, d. Richard Lark & Hester, 3 January.
Samuell, s. Samuell Symons & Dorothy, 3 January.
Mary, d. Mary Edwards, 3 January.
Thomas, s. William Butcher & Margarett, 5 January.
Alice, d. William Batty & Elizabeth, 15 January.
George, s. Arnold Wade & Mary, 10 ffebruary.

[27] Mary, d. Robert Trailane & Anne, 21 ffebruary.
Jane, d. John Gardiner, gent., & Jane, 2 March.
John, s. William Edwards & Anne, 15 March.
Thomas, s. William Levett & Susan, 16 March.
Judith, d. Henry Baily & Judith, 19 March.

1626 William, s. William Wright & Winifride, 27 March.
William, s. John Start & Jael[?], 25 April.
Thomas, s. Robert Pollard & Ellenor, 14 May.
Susan, d. Thomas Cracherode, gent., & Susan, 31 May.
Thomas, s. John Dod & Marie, 9 July.
William, s. William ffitch & Grisell, 27 July.
Edward, s. William Bigge & Meliora, 7 September.
John, s. William Cook & Grace, 24 September.
Susan, d. Daniell Newman & Christian, 10 October.
William, s. William Cason & Marie, 24 October.
Samuell, s. Robert Edwards & Katherine, 24 October.
Susan, d. John Mising & Anne, 30 October.
Ralfe, s. Ralfe Sewell & Marie, 14 January.
Nicholas, s. Thomas Piner & Marie, 16 January.

Anne, d. John Bryant & Dorcas, 4 February.
Thomas, s. John Pollard & Elizabeth, 4 ffebruary.
William, s. Thomas Trapnell & Anne, 15 ffebruary.
[28] Anna, d. Theodore Cole & Tomasin, 24 ffebruary.
John, s. John Read & Marie, 4 March.
Anne, d. Edward Wade & Margarett, 4 March.
John, s. John Purchas & Elizabeth, 10 March.
1627 George, s. George Gyps & Rebeckah, 27 March.
Harlakinden, s. Samuell Simons, gent., & Dorothy, 7 Aprill.
Thomas, s. John Gardiner, gent., & Jane, 1 May.
Mathias, s. Robert Pollard & Ellenor, 29 Julie.
John, s. Thomas Emsden & Elizabeth, 9 Sept.
Rose, d. William Pamplin & Sarah, 16 Sept.
Priscilla, d. Roger Hoiden & Sarah, 23 Sept.
Elizabeth, d. Thomas Harvie & Susan, 30 Sept.
Thomas, ye base sonne of Marie Butcher, 21 October.
Samuel, s. Samuell Bell & Elizabeth, 18 November.
Thomas, s. William Sparke & Katherine, 20 November.
Lidia, d. Samuell Hamond & Anne, 13 November.
Robert, s. John Warner & Elizabeth, 24 Januarie.
Edward, s. Edward Clay & Anne, 10 ffebruarie.
John, s. Richard Larke & Hester, 17 ffebruarie.
Giles, s. Giles Elsing & Elizabeth, 17 ffebruarie.
Thomas, s. Henry Pettit & Sarah, 21 ffebruarie.
Marie, d. Richard Edwardes & Marie, 25 ffebruarie.
[29] John, s. Arnold Wade & Marie, 25 March.
1628 Elizabeth, d. John Purchas & Elizabeth, 27 March.
Susan, d. William Smith & Anne, 1 Aprill.
Richard, s. Thomas Cracherode, gent., & Susan, 22 Aprill.
Daniell, s. John Dod & Marie, 18 May.
Bridgid, d. John Gardiner, gent., and Jane, 27 May.
John, s. John Drurie & Hester, 22 June.
Elizabeth, d. William Edwards & Anne, 10 Julie.
Robert, s. Ralfe Sewell and Marie, 17 Julie.
John, s. Samuell Simons, gent., & Dorothy, 18 Julie.
Mathias, s. Mathias Gurton & Dorothy, 27 Julie.
John, s. John Gyps, junior, & Susan, 3 August.
Marie, d. Robert Reeid & Joan, 17 August.

Thomas, s. William ffitch & Grisell, 7 September.
Jael, d. John Start & Jael, 14 September.
Martha, d. Robert Warner & Elizabeth, 9 October.
John, s. John Laver & Marie, 6 November.
Elizabeth, d. Thomas Trapnell & Anne, 6 November.
John, s. Theodore Cole & Tamesin, 18 November.
Marie, d. Ellenor Hart, widdow, 2 Januarie.
Daniell, s. John Busie & Anne, 18 Januarie.
Marie, d. William Cooke & Grace, 15 ffebruarie.
Dorcas, d. John Bryant & Dorcas, 1 March.

1629
[30] John, s. George Gyps & Rebeckah, 7 Aprill.
ffrancis, d. Richard Edwards & Marie, 26 Aprill.
Jane, d. Robert Trayland & Avis, 1 May.
Samuell, s. John Read & Marie, 5 Julie.
Richard, s. Henrie Bailie & Jjudith, 19 Julie.
Robert, s. Samuell Symons, gent., & Dorothy, 7 August.
Susan, d. John Gardiner, gent., & Jane, 18 August.
Thomas, s. Thomas Harvy & Susan, 1 October.
William, s. Elizabeth Browne, 4 October.
Susan, d. Samuell Bell & Elizabeth, 28 October.
William, s. Edward Tailer & Elizabeth, 22 November.
Dorcas, d. Robert Wentford & Marie, 1 December.
Thomas, s. Robert Pollard & Ellen, 6 December.
Marie, d. John Laver & Marie, 16 December.
William, s. William Murkin & ffrancis, 21 January.
Sarah, d. William Pamplin & Sarah, 24 Januarie.
Susan, d. Arnold Wade & Marie, 26 Januarie.
Martha, d. Henrie ffrench & Martha, 3 March.
Susan, d. John Bryant & Susan, 7 March.

1630
[31] Susan, d. John Purchas & Elizabeth, 30 March.
Daniell, s. John Start & Jael, 15 Aprill.
John, s. John Easterford & Emme, 27 May.
George, s. Thomas Trapnell & Anne, 6 June.
Anne, d. John Busie & Anne, 20 June.
John, s. John Newman & Sarah, 21 September.
Marie, d. John Gardiner, gent., & Jane, 27 October.
Sarah, d. Steven Warner & Sarah, 7 November.
William, s. Henrie Pettit & Sarah, 11 November.

Daniell, s. Barnard Sibly & ffrancis, 14 November.
Marie, d. John Anderson & Elizabeth, 28 November.
Susan, d. John Gyps, jun., & Susan, 28 November.
ffrancis, d. Richard Whiffin & ffrancis, 5 December.
Hester, d. George Gyps & Rebeckah, 12 December.
William, s. Thomas Emsden & Elizabeth, 6 Januarie.
Samuell, s. William Edwards & Anne, 24 ffebruarie.
Robert, s. William Edwards, junior, of ffullers, & Martha, 13 March.

1631 ffrancis, s. John Simpson & Elizabeth, 12 Aprill.
William, s. John Warner & Elizabeth, 21 Aprill.
[32] Anne, d. John Hale & Margarett, 24 Aprill.
Marie, d. John Bryant & Dorcas, 28 Aprill.
Hester, d. Robert Warner & Elizabeth, 12 May.
Anne, d, Robert Edwards & Luce, 12 May.
Susan, d. Thomas Pollard & Susan, 22 May.
Robert, s. Robert Wentford & Marie, 12 June.
Elizabeth, d. Theodore Cole & Tamesin, 19 June.
John, s. John ffitches, the younger, & Elizabeth, 17 Julie.
Elizabeth, d. Thomas Harvy & Susan, 31 Julie.
Susan, d. John Bellowes & Susan, 11 August.
ffrancis, d. John Busie & Anne, 29 September.
Martha, d. John Read & Maria, 16 October.
Hester, d. Richard Larke & Hester, 28 October.
Henrie, s. Henrie ffrench & Martha, 10 November.
Grace, d. John Gardiner, gent., & Jane, 16 November.
Marie, d. John Laver & Marie, 29 November.
John, s. John Purchas & Elizabeth, 19 ffebruary.
Elizabeth, d. Edward Tailer & Elizabeth, 11 March.
Lydia, d. Arnold Wade & Marie, 13 March.

[33]
1632 Susan, d. John Easterford & Emme, 27 March.
Anne, d. Thomas Trapnell & Anne, 10 May.
Elizabeth, d. Thomas Emsden & Elizabeth, 13 May.
Thomas, s. Samuel Bell & Elizabeth, 27 May.
Elizabeth, d. Edmund Drury, gent., & Elizabeth, 13 June.
William, s. Samuell Symons, gent., & Dorothy, 22 June
William, s. William Pamlin & Sarah, 22 July.

REGISTER. — BAPTISMS. 35

Samuell, s. William Cooke & Grace, 1 August.
Marie, d. John Bellowes & Susan, 16 September.
Elizabeth, d. William Butcher, junior, & Anne, 2 October.
Henry, s. William Cason & Marie, 29 May.
Dorothy, d. John Perrie, the younger, & Katherin, 7 October.
Elizabeth, d. John Anderson & Elizabeth, 28 October.
Rose, d. John Busie & Anne, 18 November.
Margaret, d. John ffisher & Allice, 18 November.
John, s. Thomas Greene & Elizabeth, 6 December.
Samuel, s. Robert Wentford & Marie, 18 December.
[34] ffrances, s. Robert Trayland & Avis, 23 December.
Thomas, s. William Redgwell & Jone, 10 ffebruary.
Richard, s. Samuell Smith & Joice, 12 ffebruary.
Katharine, d. William Chadderton & Katharine, 17 ffebruary.
Anne, d. ffrancis Martin & Marie, 19 ffebruary.
ffrancis, d. William Murkin & ffrancis, 28 ffebruary.
Anne, d. Robert Dawson & Anne, 4 March.
Grace, d. Thomas Pollard & Susan, 24 March.
1633 Anne, d. John Gardiner, gent., & Jane, 8 Aprill.
Robert, s. Peter Hale & Susan, 23 Aprill.
William, s. William Browne & Dorothy, 26 May.
Thomas, s. Thomas Warner, the younger, & Agnes, 2 June.
Marie, d. John Gyps & Susan, 9 June.
John, s. John ffitches, the younger, & Elizabeth, 2 July.
John, s. John Bryant & Dorcas, 14 July.
[35] Samuell, s. Richard Whiffin & ffrancis, 29 September.
Judith, d. Barnard Sibly & ffrancis, 29 September.
William, s. Mathew Hart & Christian, 6 October.
Marie, d. Thomas Harvy & Susan, 13 October.
James, s. James Windle & Anne, 5 November.
John, s. Thomas Sibly & Agnes, 10 November.
Sarah, d. John Start & Jael, 10 November.
Martha, d. Robert Edwards & Luce, 17 November.
Roger, s. Samuell Symons, gent., & Dorothy, 5 December.
Dorcas, d. John Laver & Marie, 12 December.

Katharin, d. Clemens Boreham, junior, & Katharin, 21 Januarie.
Richard, s. Richard Titterell, the younger, & Jone, 2 ffebruary.
Marie, d. Theodore Cole & Tamesine, 16 ffebruary.
Robert, s. Josias Pollard & Anne, 15 December.
Dorcas, d. John Read & Marie, 18 March.

[36]
1634 Margarett, d. Allice Clay, 25 March.
William, s. Thomas ffowle, gent., & Barbara, 4 May.
John, s. Richard Edwards & Marie, 3 May.
Anna, d. Anna Cresling, 20 July.
Susan, d. William Edwards & Anne, 7 August.
John, s. John Bordman & Rose, 7 September.
Sarah, d. John Easterford & Emme, 10 October.
William, s. John Perry, the younger, & Katharin, 20 October.
Susan, d. Ralfe Turner & Susan, 30 November.
Elizabeth, d. Thomas Greene & Elizabeth, 30 November.
Marie, d. Henry ffrench & Martha, 21 December.
Marie, d. John ffisher & Allice, 28 December.
Anne, d. John Dollar & Anne, 28 December.
William, s. John Bryant & Dorcas, 29 January.
Marie, d. William Warner & Marie, 29 January.

[37] Henrie, s. John Busie & Anne, 2 ffebruary.
John, s. William Pamplin & Sara, 8 ffebruary.
Marie, d. ffrancis Martin & Mary, 5 March.

1635 Thomas, s. Thomas Pollard & Susan, 30 Aprill.
Samuell, s. Thomas Emsden & Elizabeth, 14 May.
Richard, s. Thomas ffowle, gent., & Barbara, 2 June.
Martha, d. William Browne & Dorothy, 30 June.
Marie, d. Nathanaell Paul & Marie, 19 Julie.
Lydia, d. William Edwards, of ffullers, & Lydia, 18 August.
Tabitha, d. John Anderson & Elizabeth, 23 August.
Anne, d. William Redgewell & Jone, 23 August.
Jonas, s. James Windle & Anne, 17 September.
John, s. John Bellowes & Susan, 27 September.
Anne, d. Thomas Warner & Agnes, 4 October.

[38] Elizabeth, d. Nathanael Thurston, gent., & Marie, 9 October.
John, s. William Murkin & ffrancis, 11 October.
Thomas, s. Thomas Roote & Anna, 10 November.
Anna, d. Edward Tailer & Elizabeth, 22 November.
William, s. Robert Edwards & Luce, 29 December.
Susan, d. Thomas Harvy & Susan, 13 December.
Steven, s. Steven Warner & Sara, 27 December.
ffrancis, d. Thomas Edwards & Elizabeth, 21 ffebruary
ffrancis, reputed son of Thomas Smith & Margaret his wyfe, 13 March.
William, s. Henrie Smith & Sara, 15 March.
Marie, d. Thomas Trapnell & Anne, 15 March.
ffrancis Gall is my name and eeigth son of ———*

1636 John, s. Samuell Bateman & Elizabeth, 10 Aprill.
Clemens, s. Clemens Borham, junior, & Katharine, 19 Aprill.
Richard, s. John Gyps & Susan, 5 May.
Marie, d. William Greene & Marie, 15 May. [May.
[39] Olive, d. John Perrie, the younger, & Katharine, 29
Mathew, s. John ffitches & Elizabeth, 29 June.
John, s. John Titterell & Dorcas, 3 July.
Marie, d. Robert Wentford & Marie, 14 August.
Sara, d. Thomas Wood & Sara, 4 September.
Elizabeth, d. Richard Titterill & Jone, 25 September.
Robert, s. Robert Maltiward, gent., & Elizabeth, 1 October.
Ann, d. William Cooke & Grace, 15 October.
Ann, d. Richard Whiffer & ffrancys, 23 October.
Ann, d. William Mere & Sara, 28 October.
Richard, s. Josias Pollard & Anne, 1 November.
William, s. Thomas Greene & Elizabeth, 15 December
Thomas, s. George Earles & Elizabeth, 1 January.
John, s. John ffisher & Alice, 8 January.
Mary, d. William Browne & Dorothy, 18 January.
Rebecca, d. Elizabeth Sparke, base born, 4 February.
John, s. John Kinge & Margarett, 10 February.
Dorothy, d. ffrancis Martin & Mary, 5 March.
Elizabeth, d. Michael Richardson, jun., & Mary, 16 March.

---
*The rest of the entry is blotted and illegible.

1637 John, s. John Bryant & Dorcas, 11 April.
[40] Benjamin, s. John Reade & Mary, 25 April.
Susan, d. Thomas Mathews & Susan, 15 May.
Sara, d. Henry Smith & Sara, 30 May.
Robt., s. John Esterford & Emmey, 23 July.
Thomas, s. John Start & Jael, 27 August.
Robt., s. Robt. Edwards, jun., & *Luce, 17 Septemb.
William, s. John Bellowes & Susan, "the same day and year."
Elizabeth, d. John Busie & Anne, 29 Octob.
William, s. William Redgewell & Joane, 12 Novemb.
Thomas, s. Robt. Maltiward, gent., & Elizabeth, 26 Novemb.
Mary, d. Thomas Roote & Anna, 3 Decemb.
Robert, s. John Laver & Mary, 21 Decemb.
Mary, d. William Murkin & Frances, 17 Decemb.
William, s. William Borde, 28 Decemb.
John, s. Henry Ewins & Susan, 18 Janu.
Dorothy, d. Thomas Harvey & Susan, 21 Janu.
Samuell, s. Thomas Emsden, 12 Feb.
Robert, s. Clement Borham & Catherine, 4 March.
1638 Mary, d. Michael Richardson, jun., & Mary, 15 April.
Anne, d. William Smith & Margaret, the same day.
John, s. Josias Pollard & Anna, 29 June.
John, s. John Overed, Clerke & Christian, 3 July.
Samuel, s. Samuel Bateman, the younger, & Hannah, 29 August.
Thomas, s. John Gyps & Susan, 28 August.
John, s. Thomas ffowle, gent., & Margaret, 2 Septem.
William, s. William† & Margaret, 27 Septem.
Mary, d. William Alston, gent., & Mary, 27 Septem.
[41] Timothie, s. John Kinge & Margaret, the day aforesaid
William, s. William Greene & Mary, 15 Octob.
Anna, d. Richard Kempe & Mary, 11 Octob.
Mary, d. Henry Smith & Sarah, 5 Novemb.
Henry, s. Henry Laver & Mary, 15 Novemb.
William, s. John ffitches & Elizabeth, 13 Decemb.
Mary, d. William Borham & Margaret, 6 Janu.

---
*The name Elizabeth is erased.
†The name is much rubbed, the first letter is H, the end is plainly *iball*, and the whole name probably *Huddiball*.

Henery, s. Thomas Greene & Elizabeth, 13 Janu.
Jonathan, s. Thomas Roote & Anna, 2 Feb.
Martha, d. Laurence More & Martha, 17 Feb.
Mathew, s. Richard Edwards & Mary, 19 Feb.
———, –. Edward Taylor & Elizabeth, 25 Feb.
Elizabeth, d. Robt. Malteward, gent., & Elizabeth, 5 March.

1639 Elizabeth, d. Thomas Cornell & Katherin, 30 March.
Richard, s. Richard Cant & Elizabeth, 16 April.
Dorcas, d. John Titterill & Dorcas, 11 May.
Thomas, s. Martin Olley & Anne, 23 May.
———, d. Richard Cobb, 16 September.
Susan, d. Thomas Woode & Sarah, 20 September.
Samuel, s. Samuel Bateman, jun., 20 October.
Dorcas, d. Henery Laver, jun., & Mary, 27 Octob.
Mathias, baseborn child of Susan Shedd, 19 Novemb.
Elizabeth, d. John Overed, Clerk & Christian, 20 Novem
Mary, d. Oliver Keene & May, 26 December.
ffrances, d. John Briant & Dorcas, 14 January.
Hannah, d. Thomas Mathewes & Susan, the same day.
Samuel, s. John Weeber & ffrances, 26 January.
Moses, s. Moses Harrington, 23 Feb.
Margaret, d. John Kinge & Margaret, 23 Feb.
Grace, d. Gabriel Shedd & Agnes [?], 28 Feb.

[42] Martha, d. Michael Richardson, jun., & Ann, 8 March.
Daniel, s. Daniel Gurten, 8 March.
Mary, d. John Esterford & Emvira, the same day.
Dorothy, d. John ffisher & Alice, 10 March.
Henery, s. Henery Smith & Sarah, 12 March.
Anne, baseborn child of Anna Winterfloud, 23 March.
Martha, d. John Bellowes & Susanah, 4 August.

1640 William, s. William Redgewell & Joane, 4 April.
Robert, s. Robt. Right & Mary, 7 April.
———, d. Richard Titterill, 20 May.
John, s. —— Anderson & Elizabeth, 31 May.
Peter, s. Thomas Warner & Anne, 5 July.
Hester, d. James Chaplyn & Hester, 12 August.
Joseph, s. William Murkin & ffrances, 27 Septemb.
Thomas, s. Richard Kempe & Mary, 28 Octob.
Margaret, d. William Huddiball & Margaret, 15 Nov.

Mary, d. Robert Ailcoke & Elizabeth, 20 November.
Elizabeth, d. Laurence More & Martha, 29 Novemb.
William, s. Richard Whiffin & ffrances, 6 Demb. [*sic.*]
Robert, s. Richard Cant & Elizabeth, 31 January.
Thomas, s. Thomas Woode, 7 March.
Mary, d. William Bacon & Mary, 9 March.

1641 John, s. Dennis Elye & Sarah, 28 March.
Samuel, s. Samuel Bateman, the elder, & Elizabeth, April 27.
Thomas, s. Samuel Bateman, the younger, & Hannah, the same day.
Samuell, s. Robert Lynsell & Barbara, last day of May.
Jane, d. Robert Mathew & Margaret, 21 June.
Susanna, d. William Alstone, gent., & Mary, 25 Sept.
Anne, d. Marten Olley, 10 Octob.
Michael, reputed s. Mihill Brewster, baseborn of —— Quy, 28 Octob.
Hanna, d. James Knidall & Hanna, 20 July.

[43] Anne, d. Edward Tayler, November.
Susanna, d. William Smith, December 6.
Elizabeth, d. John Kinge & Margaret, December 25.
John, s. John Weeke & Frances, Jan. 26.
Robert, s. Robert Edwards & Mary, Feb. 20.
Thomas, s. Richard Kempe, Oct. 10.
Elizabeth, d. Oliver Keene & Mary, 2 day Feb.

1642 William, s. William Raven, Feb. 20.
Mary, d. Jeremy Piper, Aprill 2.
Samuel, s. Samuel Bridge, April 20.
James, s. James Chaplyn, April 23.
Mary, d. Thomas Mathews, April 26.
Elizabeth, d. John Stone, April 28.
Joseph, s. William Warner & Mary, June 24.
Martha, d. Clement Boreham, & Katheren, 2 Octob.
Anne, d. Thomas Cornell & Katheran, 19 October.
William, s. William Alston, gent., & Mary, 5 Feb.
James, s. James Shed, 5 Feb.
Anne, d. Laurance Moor, 23 March.

1643 Mary, d. Thomas Emsden & Elizabeth, 10 May.
James, s. James Kendall & Johannah, 6 August.
Elizabeth, d. William Smith & Elizabeth, 20 October.

REGISTER. — BAPTISMS. 41

William, s. Robert Edwards & Mary, 24 October.
Rose, d. Nathan Bateman, 28 October.
Sarah, d. Thomas Cornell & Katheran, 25 July.
Abigail, d. Richard Kemp, 15 Decemb.
Jemima, d. William Alston, gent., & Mary, Feb. 12.
Elizabeth, d. John Esterford & Emery, Feb. 26.
ffrancis Gall.

1644 Susan, d. Martin Olly & Anne, June 7.
William, s. William Warner & Mary, June 18.
[44] James, s. James Chaplin & Esther, July 2.
Mary, d. Nathan Bateman & Rose, Sept. 12.   [30.
Thomas, s. Mordant Cratchrood & Dorothy, Novemb.
Thomas, s. Thomas Edward & Hannah, Janu. 5.
John, s. Henry Laver, senior, & Mary, feb. 2.
Henry, s. Henry Gyps, feb. 18.
Hannah, d. John Bellows, Feb. 28.

1645 Elizabeth, d. William Raven, April 8.
Elizabeth, d. Edward Earle & Katherin, April 14.
Robert, s. Henry Laver, junior, & Susan, feb. 20.
Sarah, d. John Start, jun., and Avis, May 4.
Thomas, s. Thomas Green & Anne, 12 May.
Martha, d. William Smith & Margarett, June 4.
William, s. William Smith & Elizabeth, July 8.
Elizabeth, d. William Raven & Mary, Oct. 7.
William, s. William Mathew & Anne, Oct. 20.
Robert, s. Henry Eivens & Alice, Feb. 10.
[45] Mary, d. John Overed, minister, & Penelope, 24 May.
Cornelius, s. Oliver Reave & Mary, 28 May.
Mary, d. Robert Edwards & Mary, the same day.
ffrances, d. William Green & Mary, June 12.
Margaret, d. Robert Butcher, 2 July.
Laurance, s. Laurance Moor & Martha, 12 July.
Joanna, d. Robert Gurton, 27 July.
Martha, d. Richard Kemp, 27 December.
Thomas, s. William Huddeball, 16 January.

1646 Anne, d. Thomas Edwards & Anne, 6 April.
Jeremiah, s. Jeremiah Piper & Sarah, 20 June.
John, s. Clement Boreham & Katherin, 26 June.
Grace, d. Moses Harrington, 17 May.
Elizabeth, d. Thomas Borham, Octob.

Jonathan, s. John Overed, minister, & Penelope, 29 August.
Robert, s. Richard Titterill, 2 October.
Susan, d. Thomas Emsden & Elizabeth, June 24.
John, s. George Earle & Katherin, Sept. 29.
Joanna, d. John Alston, gent., Sept. 21. [tob.
Anthony, s. Mordant Cratchrood & Dorothy, 23 Oc-
John, s. John Start and Avis, Septemb. 6.
Thomas, s. Robert Butcher, Septemb. 15.
Thomas, s. Thomas Simson, 26 febr.
John, s. Richard Pepper, 5 March.
Robert, s. William Edwards & Elizabeth, 25 January.
John, s. Robert Edwards & Mary, 10 Novemb.

[46] Henry, s. Henry Laver, junior, & Susan, 20 March.
William, s. Richard Warner & Rachell, 18 March.

1647 Sarah, d. John Overed & Penelope, 30 June.
Robert, s. Michael Brewster, 2 August.
William, s. William Deeks, 12 August.
Robert, s. Robert Earle & Mary, Sept. 5.
Robert, s. Robert Pollard & Abigail, Sept. 20.
Sarah, d. Dennis Ely & Sarah, Dec. 27.
Robert, s. Christopher Erle, Esq.,* & Mary, February 19.
John, s. Robert Rust & Mary, February 27.

---

*This name is found elsewhere. Leland Duncan, Esq., F. S. A., writes: "I see that in one of the appendices to Dr. Shaw's 'History of the Church of England during the Commonwealth,' Toppesfield is spelt Topfield." He gives the name of the man who was intruded into the rectory and names of the "elders".——10 July, 1648, Mr. Overed to topesfield, Essex. Commons Journals, vol. v., p. 651; Lords Journals, x, p. 404.

An attempt was made to divide Essex into "Classes" for Presbyterian purposes. The 10th. Classis, called the Classis of Hincford, contained "Topfield," minister, Mr. Jo. Overed; Elders, Christopher Earle, Esq., Mr. Samuel Smith, and Robert Wentford. All these names are found in the register.

John Overed (erroneously called Thomas in the list of rectors exhibited in Toppesfield Church, and in copies made from that list) is first described in the registers as Clerke. He was a curate in charge of the parish during the time that Dr. Burnell was rector, the name of his wife at this time was Christian. She died (burials, Nov. 20, 1639), he afterwards married Penelope (May 24, 1643), where he is first described as minister. Probably he received the Rectory as a reward for his religious pliancy.

REGISTER. — BAPTISMS. 43

         ffrancis Gall.
1648   ffrancis Gall.
John, s. Jeremiah Piper & Mary, June 20. [24.
Hannah, d. John Overed, minister, & Penelope, July
Daniel, s. Daniel Richardson & Rachel, May 10.
John, s. Thomas Green and Anne, June 28.
Thomas, s. Thomas Miller & Mary, July 4.
Thomas, s. Thomas Boreham & Elizabeth, July 5. [7.
Mary, d. Morduant Cracherood, gent., & Dorothy, July
Solomon, s. William Alston, gent., & Mary, July 18.
William, s. Samuel Bridge & Mercy, August 28.
John, s. Richard Titterell, Sept. 20.
Margaret, d. Thomas Matthew, Oct. 29.
[47] Mary, d. James Shed, January 2. [June.
1649 Penelope, d. John Overed, minister, & Penelope, 29
Matthew, s. Matthew Edwards & Ann, 12 May.
Elizabeth, d. John Pollard & Elizabeth, June 20.
Thomas, s. Thomas Green, June 21.
Philip, s. Thomas Winterflood & Mary, July 7.
Anne, d. John Smith & Margaret, Aug. 30.
Joseph, s. Richard Warner & Rachell, Feb. 5.
Daniel, s. Henry Laver & Susan, Janu. 1.
William, s. William Wright, Janu. 7. [27.
1650 Morduant, s. Morduant Cratchrood & Dorothy, March
Thomasin, d. William Edwards & Elizabeth, May 2.
Elizabeth, d. John Alston, gent., May 15.
Ann, d. Thomas Green, June 23.
Thomas, s. Moses Harrington, July 20.
Sarah, d. Edward Bointell & Sarah, Dec. 10.
Elizabeth, d. William Matthew & Ann, Dec. 15.
Samuel, s. Thomas Miller & Mary, Jan. 9.
John, s. John Stanes & Hester, the same day.
Samuel, s. Daniel Richardson & Rachell, Jan. 16.
John, s. Samuel Bridge & Mercy, Jan. 20.
Dorcas, reputed daughter of William Berd & baseborn
  of Dorcas Drury, July 10.
John, s. John Seaman & Rebecca, 12 July.
Samuel, s. Robert Earles & Mary, 6 August.
John, s. Thomas Simson & Margaret, feb. 18.

MARRIAGES.

[72]
1560 John Cirke & Ellin Buttall, 9 May.
William Pollard & Margaret Lende, 23 May.
Steven Titterell & Elizabeth Maysant, 27 May.
1561 Thomas ffytchs & Katherine Rayner, 7 December.
Michael Tongue & Alice Alwin, 3 October.
1562 Christopher ffiche & Joane Browne, 8 June.
Robert Edward & Marie Parker, 15 August.

The above seven entries are written (evidently copied) on the bottom of a page of baptisms; the next leaf has been cut out.

ffrancis Gall.   Churchwarden.
ffor Yearre 1688.

[75]
1598 George Rule & Joane Wells, 30 April.
Richard Titterell & Anne Thetford, 22 June.
William Roger & Sarah Wast, 26 November.
1599 John Clarke of Radwinter, wid., & Margerie Berding single w., 11 April.
William Snelling & Margaret Chatwood, 10 August.
John Bayly, widd. & Mary Tilbish, widdowe, 29 August.
John Choate & Mary Grettit, 8 January.
Henry Smith & Mother Coozin, 10 December.
Robert Spiltimber & Thomasin Boultin, 19 October.
1600 David Playle & Margarett Lamson, 21 April.
Edmund Cant & Grace Welles, 8 May.
Henry Cirke & Rebecca Aylett, 28 October.
1601 Michael Clerk & Margaret Webb, 28 Octobe.

(44)

REGISTER. — MARRIAGES. 45

	Robert Clerke & Joanne Trappe, 30 January.
1602	Samuell Edwards & Cicely Big, 7 November.
1603	Thomas Wilcocke & Ann Brown, 1 November.
	Jeffry Harvy & Rebecca Cirk, 7 November.
	James Weager & Lettice Bunting, 5 November.
	John Smyth & Mary Edwards, 20 ffebruary.
1604	Josiah Collin & Elizabeth Amis, 20 April.
	Robert Edwarde & Elizabeth Warner, 8 May.
	Widdow^r. Brown & Christian Pettit, 24 Julie.
	John Cooke & Mary Horrold, 7 October.
1603	James Tayler & Triphena Borham, 23 August, 1603.
1604	Thomas Chatterton & Rose Perry, 16 January.
1605	Thomas Dawkins & Agnes Hart, 1 May.
	Henry Snelhok & Goane Chapman, 7 May.
	William Evans & Anne Wastell, 16 July.
	Thomas Mathew, alias Micke, & Margery Boram, 4 August. [gust.
	John Crawborrow & Ellen Evanfeill, widdow, 29 Au-
	Clement Borham & Lucy Crawborrow, 28 October.
	John Pollard and Alice Edwards, 27 ffebruary.
1606	Henry French & Anne Perry, 13 July.
	Thomas Horrold & Mary Cosin, 14 October.
	John Brande & Mary Buttoll, Nov. 27.
	John Godwin & Penelope Evered, Jan. 8.
1607	John Quye & Sara Shedd, April 18.
	John Watson & Christian Reede, Sept. 14.
	Thomas Clearkson & Mary Jolly, Sept. 28.
	Jeremye Paxman & Elizabeth Reede, Oct. 8.
	Richard Hamond & Joan Leony, Oct. 18.
1608	Henry Laver & Mathewe ———, June 30.
	John Mayor & Elizabeth Everid, July 22.
	Roger Ale & Margaret Browne, July 29.
	George Lowimyr & Mary Bunting, Oct. 9.
	Henry Petitte & Sara Edwards, Nov. 3.
[76]	Thomas Javleton & Clement Bennet, Novemb. 30.
1609	John Wallaker & Margaret Warner, January 22.
	William Overed & Mathew Bateman, January 23.
1610	John Gofeild & ffrancis Edwarde, 7 May.
	John Bernard & Elizabeth Jollie, 2 Julye. [ber.
	Robert Perry & Elizabeth Chamberlayne, 24 Septem-

TOPPESFIELD, ENGLAND, PARISH

        Laurence More & Elizabeth Gippe, 13 October.
1611 Philip Anstell & Alse Edward, 27 May.
        Thomas Gooddin & Margeret George, 1 July.
        Samuel Bateman & Mary Berdin, 8 August.
1612 Thomas Onion & Debora Bateman, 21 April.
        Nathan Bateman & Marie Livermore, 24 June.
        Arthur Winterfloud & Clement Jurden, 3 August.
        William Ward & Elizabeth Billiwood, alias Bust, 20 Sept.
1613 Edward Riche & Susan Warner, November 1.
        John Clarke & Rose Laver, March 7.
1614 Gregory Warner & Elizabeth Edwards, May 8.
        John Dod & Mary Amye, May 12.
        John Ewer & Anne Lawer, May 29.
1615 Richard Gips & Susan Bateman, May 13.
        Samuel Bland & Elizabeth Harvey, May 18.
        Jeremie Pearman & Thomasin French, June 23.
        William Cooke & Grace Cant, Julie 23.
        Thomas Brewar & Susan Edwards, Jan. 9.
1616 Giles Elzing & Elizabeth Hide, April 25.
        William Edwards & Anne Parke, May 27.
1617 Peter Hall & Susan Brian, Oct. 23.
        John Simpson & Elizabeth ffarrar, June 18.
        George Gurton & Alice Cirke, June 23.
        Robert Frost & Judith Sibly, Oct. 28.
        Ambrose Tompson & Thomasin Gips, November 9.
        Thomas Andrews & Katherene Bragg, June 23.
1618 Thomas Bromley & Martha Webb, May 7.
        Samuell Wike & Anne Sible, May 21.
        Samuell Edwards & ffrances Greene, June 24.
        Daniel Smith & Tomazin Smith, July 2.
        William ffitch & Grisell Holton, Oct. 23.
[77] Thomas Ruggles & Elizabeth Barnard, Octob. 6.
        Hercules Evans & Alice Cant, Nov. 5.
        Henry Smith & Sarar Bigg, Nov. 23.
        John Clay & Joane Rudland, wid., Jan 12.
        Edward Bateman & Prudence Mosse, ff. 9.
1619 John Prackett & Thomazin Cordar, July 8.
        July 31. Joseph Jackson & Margarett Read.
        Sept. 27. Jhon ffisher & Bridgett Leman.

REGISTER. — MARRIAGES. 47

   Sept. Richard Larke & Esther Cornhill.
   Feb. 2. Raphe Sewell & Marie Butcher were buried[?].
1620 Sept. 29. Steven Waterworth & Alice Amie.
   Nov. 28. John Start & Alice Dod, wid.
   Jan. 28. Edward Mariott & Ester Bateman.
1621 April 19. William Browne & Anne Pettit.
   John Most & Elizabeth Selling, 6 July.
   Edward West & Alline Hostler, 2 August.
1622 John Read & Mary Warner, 10 June.
   William Wright & Winifred Plaile, 24 June.
1623 Arnold Wade & Mary Bateman, 25 Aprill.
   John Mising & Anne Cooke, 24 July.
   William Butcher & Anne ffurmin, 2 Octobe. [ber.
   Jeremie Pearmaine & Tamesin Thompson, 2 Novem-
1624 Jeremie Sansum & Lidia ffinch, 6 Aprill.
   Elias Rayner & Barbara Tongue, 1 August.
   Thomas Read & ffrances Tompson, 28 November.
1625 John Start & Elizabeth Baily, 5 ffebruary. [ruary.
[78] Robert Grant, alias Bryant & Elizabeth Hog, 21 ffeb-
1626 John Perrie & Rose Humfrey, Nov. 1.
1627 Joseph Jackson & Thomasin Chamberlaine, 2 August.
   Mathias Gurton & Dorothie Hog, 5 November.
   John Bellowes & Anne Start, 17 Januarie.
1628 Richard Wright & Dinah Smith, 4 August.
1629 Richard Lot & Rose Bun, 7 May.
   Thomas Randoll & Barbara Davie, 21 Sept.
   Robert Edwards & Luce Siblie, 29 Sept.
   Robert Stevens & Ellen Hart, 5 October.
   Henrie Gyps & Elizabeth Harrington, 24 November.
   Richard Shellie & Elizabeth Start, 24 Januarie.
1630 John ffisher & Allice Smith, 8 July.
   John Turner & Anna Cole, 12 Julie.
   John Dollar & Anne Browne, 10 August.
   John ffitches & Elizabeth Greene, 7 October.
1631 William Edwards, of ffullers, & Rachell Bridge, 15 November.
   Henry Clarke & Clemens Winterfloud, 20 November.
   John Onyon & Elizabeth Smith, 20 Januarie.
1632 Thomas Warner & Anne Greene, 11 June.

48 TOPPESFIELD, ENGLAND, PARISH

John Jaggard & Susan Roote, 3 January.

[79]
1633 John Bordman & Rose Drury, 22 July.
John Skelie & Dorothy Butcher, 25 July.
William Warner & Marie Edward, 15 August.
John King & Anne Kendall, 8 October. [May.
1634 Robert Mathew, alias Wix, & Margarett Boote, 27
William Greene & Marie Lithermore, 6 November.
William Board & Sarah Argent, 24 January.
1635 Thomas Birkner & Sara Wood, 30 Aprill.
William Clarke & ffrances Edward, 30 July.
Robert Maltiward & Elizabeth Cracherode, 26 August.
Henrie Holton & Margarett Evans, 29 September.
Nicholas Argent & Marie Titterell, 20 October.
William Perrie & Abigail Hancock, 28 October.
1636 Thomas Wood & Sara Shed, 28 November.
Henry Evens & Susan Ostler, 17 October.
John Parmane, the younger, & Elizabeth Butcher, 8 October.
1637 Thomas Bacon & Priscilla Badcocke, 20 April.
William Huddiball & Margaret Shed, last day of November.

[80]
1638 John Wicks & ffrances Perrye, 19 October.
George Sharp & Mary Drury, 23 October.
Nathaniel Kent & Anne Turner, 5 November.
Nathan ffrogg & Joane Griggs, 24 January.
1639 Robert Rust & Mary Bateman, 23 May.
Henry May & Elizabeth Harding, 24 June.
Aron Butcher & Elizabeth Edwards, 30 October.
1640 William Winterflood & Anne Butcher, June 10.
Dennys Elye & Sarah Edwards, June 24.
James Kindall & Hannah ——, Aug. 28.
Richard Newman & Mary Pereman, December 20.
1642 John Willoughby, gent., & Margaret his wife were marryed April 20. [1649.
1647 John Newman, widdower, & Sarah Hogg, Sept. 29.
Space of nearly half a page blank, and the first entry on the next page is dated 1654.

BURIALS.

[83]
1560 Simon Eesborow was buried the 6th. day of April in the yeere of O. L. God 1560.
John Purkas, 7 februarie.
1561 Elioner Maught, 13 februarie.
Christopher Harvie, 21 februarie.
Margaret May, 23 februarie.
Thomas Harvie, 28 februarie.
1562 Agnes ffiche, 12 April.
Agnes ffiche, the daughter, 23 May.
1563 Alice Berd, 30 December.
Anne Plomb, 5 Januarie.
1564 Agnes ffrench, 6 April.
Barbara Tongue, 22 June.
Thomas Plomb, 2 Septeber.
John Rizing, 17 Septeber.
Richard Yeldam, 25 Septeber.
Robert Pollard, 1 October.
John Thetford, 22 Deceber.
Rose Edward, 20 Januarie.
1565 Alyce Gaskyn, 13 October.
William Tongue, 4 Januarie.
Alyce Garroulde, 25 Januarie.
1566 Elizabeth Tyttrylle, 28 March.
Anne Farthing, 17 August.
Elizabeth Rawlinge, 23 Septeber.
John Hayward, 4 Noveber.
Katherine Gridley, 23 Januarie.
John Pollard, 9 Februarie.

Thomas Plomb, the elder, 19 Februarie.
1567 Henrie Bust, 1 April.
Joane Butcher, 2 Julie.
Richard Underwood, 11 August.
William Hamont, 3 October.
William Humfrie, 28 October.
Elizabeth Adcocke, 9 Noveber.
Joane Hulle, 18 Februarie.
1568 Anne Browne, 26 March.
John Mote, s. William Mote, last day of March.
Briget, d. Heugh Rawling, last day of March.
Alyce, d. Thomas Hybys, 14 April.
Katherine, d. Thomas Hybys, 17 April.
Barbara, d. John Greene, 23 April.
Richard, s. Henrie Thelford, last day of April.
Ane, the wife of Nicholas Warde, 8 November.
Elizabeth, d. William Edward, 2 Januarie.
Elizabeth, d. Henrie Reade, 16 Februarie.
1569 Elizabeth, d. Thomas Adcocke, 18 April.
John, s. John Harrington, 17 August.
Joane Adams, widowe, alias Butcher, 14 October.
Plesance, d. Edward Richardson, 21 December.
1570 Ane, d. Christopher Fitch, 3 Septeber.
Grace, d. Thomas Cracherood, 15 September.
John Craneford, servant, 6 October.
Edward, s. Christopher ffitch, 21 Januarie.
Richard Perrye, of flowers Hall, 23 Januarie.
Alyce, d. Henrie Snellocke, 1 ffebruarie.
Katherine, d. John Harrington, 19 Februarie.
Edmund, s. Robert Turner, 16 March.
1571 Richard, s. Richard Mote, 12 Maye.
John, s. William Mortemer, last day of Maye.
Ane, d. William Mortemer, 18 June.
Samuel, s. William Edward, 22 June.
Peter, s. William Stebbinge, 21 Julie.
Agnes Rizing, widowe, 29 December.
George, s. John Bust, 3 Januarie.
John, s. John Edward, the elder, 13 Januarie.
[84] Alyce, the servant to Robert Briant, 28 Januarie.
Henrie Reade, 16 Februarie.

REGISTER. — BURIALS. 51

1572 Joane Mortemer, wid., 26 March.
Joane, w. John Skeltie, 3 June.
Steven Tittrill, 3 Julie.
Thomas, s. John Cozin, 8 September.
Margerie, w. James Snellocke, last day of October.
Marie, d. Thomas Cracherood, the elder, 20 february.

1573 John Odye, servant, 3 May.
Phillys, d. Richard Everide, 18 May.
Nichobas Warde, wide., 18 August.
William, s. Hugh Rawling, 20 August.
Richard, s. Paule Rawling, 9 September.
ffrancis, s. Richard Yeldam, 24 September.
Rose, d. Thomas Spiltimber, 4 November.
Margaret Gips, wid., 8 December.

1574 Joane Smitton, wid., 14 April.
Alyce, w. William Reade, 14 Maye.
Richard, s. William Edward, 25 October.
John Reade, the bas: 12 Deceb.

1575 John, s. Richard Hulle, 26 April.
Alyce, w. William Stebbing, 24 Julie.
Robert, s. William Reade, 24 September.
Thomas Grene, 12 Novemb.

1576 John Cracherood, 3 Januarie.
Thomas Caunts, 15 Januarie.
Robert Bryne, 15 Februarie.
Nicholas Belle, servant, 10 Maye.
Thomas Spiltimber, 12 June.
Alyce, w. William Pollard, last day of June.

1577 Thomas Pollard, 2 Julie.
Elizabeth Sanders, servant, 30 October.
Anne, d. Henrie Smith, 1 November.
William Bateman, 1 Deceber.
Christopher Fitch, 18 Januarie.

1579 John Hamond, 20 June.

1580 Henrie, s. Henrie Smith, 29 Maye.
Joane Pollard, widowe, 1 November.
Elizabeth Titrell, widowe, 4 November.
ffrances Humfrie, 6 Noveber.
Henrie Harrington, 17 Noveber.
Richard Denis, a stranger, 26 November.

1581 Margaret, d. Thomas Bateman, 25 Julie.
John Browne, the elder, 9 August.
Samuel Bigg, 24 August.
Margaret Pollard, 20 November.
Richard Yeldam, 27 Noveber.
Henrie Thetford, 27 Februarie.
1582 Ambrose Sparowe, 12 April.
[85] Barbara, w. Henrie Snellock, the elder, 27 June.
Elizabeth, d. Henrie Snellocke, the elder, 14 Julie.
James, s. John Harrington, yeoman, 7 September.
John Francis, 4 Noveber.
1583 Anne, w. John Bosall, 19 May.
Anne, w. Thomas Bosall, 11 June.
Anne Briant, widow, 20 June.
Christian, d. Robert Edward, 7 August.
Widowe Constable, 15 August.
1584 Elizabeth, w. John Harrington.
Elizabeth Richardson, 24 August.
Alyce, w. Richard Mote, 4 Septeber.
The wife of Edward Hampton, 22 November.
Thomas Edward, 17 Deceber.
John Edward, 29 Januarie.
The wife of William Pollard, 1 Februarie.
1585 Joane, w. William Mortimer, 3 April.
Alyce Spiltimber, 16 April.
Alyce Browne, widow, 1 May.
Margerie, w. William Harrington, 24 May.
Frances Barnes, 5 June.
John Bacon, 2 November.
William Mortimer, 3 November.
Henrie Bateman, 8 November.
William Cracherood, the elder, 12 Januarie.
William Bigge, 26 Januarie.
1586 Roger Brewster, servant, 30 April.
John Plume, 1 October.
Richard Snellocke, 1 Deceber.
Anne, w. Henrie Smith, 12 December.
Anne Bever, 14 December.
Alyce, d. John Percy, 11 March.
1587 William Bosall, 15 Julie.

Joane, w. Robert George, 8 September.
John Syke, last day of October.
Alyce Tittryll, 8 Noveber.
The wife of John Warman, 12 November.
John Hamond, 12 Noveber.
Thomas Whiting, 3 December.
Elizabeth Cracherood, widow, 15 februarie.
Mother Harrington, widow, 2 March.

1588 John Gipps, 27 Julie.
Katherine Tonge, widow, 12 Januarie.
Joseph, s. Lewes Bret, 15 Januarie.

[86] John Bust, 10 Februarie.
John Pollard, 13 March.
Robert Cartwright, 27 April.
Thomas, s. Henrie Smith, 8 May.
Marian Reade, widow, 10 August.
——— Tylbroke, 11 Noveber.
Matthew Edward, 27 Noveber.
Elizabeth Bosall, 1 March.

1590 Edee Easkin, w. Richard Easkin, 13 May.
Katherine ffrancis, widow, 2 June.
Sarah Hamond, d. John Hamond, 29 Januarie.
Anne Hamond, 12 March.

1591 John Browne, 2 Julie.
Thomas Bateman, 10 Julie.
William Bocher, 10 October.
Julian Adcoke, 20 October.
John Bird, of flowers hall, 28 November.
ffrancis Bird, 13 Deceber.

1592 Richard Easkin, 29 Septeber.
Sarah Turner, 7 Januarie.
A poore pedler man, 7 Januarie.
The two yonge daughters of William Edward, of Brad-
  fields, were burid the fifth day after their birth.

1593 Anne, d. Widow Greene, 18 May.
Rose, w. Henrie Snellock, the younger, 14 Julie.
Katherine Thorowgood, 24 August.
Alyce, w. Michael Tongue, 28 September.
Joane, d. Thomas Cracherood, 20 October.
A daughter of Thomas Hurrell, 20 October.

54 TOPPESFIELD, ENGLAND, PARISH

      John Bayle, miller, 1 Deceber.
      Sarah Tyler, 17 December.
1594 Henrie, s. Richard Mote, 19 August.
      Joane, w. William Bocher, 22 August.
      Alyce, w. John Cozen, 15 September.
      William, s. William Thorogood, 3 December.
      Henrie, s. John Reade, 25 December.
      William Allin, last day of January.
      Joseph, s. Ishak Cornwell, 17 March.
1595 John Harrington, 2 April.
      Robert Lambe, a stranger, 19 April.
      The wife of Robert Tongue, 19 May.
      Elizabeth, w. William Edward, 28 May.
      John Posler, 3 June.
      William Reade, 5 June.
[87] ffather Kempe, 28 June.
      Jerome Turtell, 5 December.
      Margerie Bosall, 5 December.
      The child of Lewes Brett, 7 December.
      Widow Bayle, 11 March.
1596 Margaret King, widow, 17 October.
      A poore begger woman, 26 December.
      Thomas Buttall, 3 Januarie.
      Cicelye Bust, widow, 10 Januarie.
      Marie, d. Henry Snellock, 25 februarie.
      John, s. John Fiche, 6 January.
1597 Thomas Smillon, 1 May.
      The widow of John Browne, 10 June.
      John Cosen, 28 Julie.
      Alyce, w. Richard Mote, 29 August.
      John Humfrie, 6 September.
      Angela Byford, 10 December.
      Elizabeth Coe, 14 December.
      Richard Cowlet, 2 Januarie.
      William Turtell, 12 Januarie.
      Alyce, w. George Rule, 15 Januarie.
      Margaret, w. John Hewes, 16 Februarie.
      William Whiting, parson of Toppesfield, 22 Februarie.
      Susan, d. Edmund Whiting, 1 March.
      Alyce Rysing, 19 March.

REGISTER. — BURIALS.

1598 Alyce Greene, widow, 25 March.
Anne, d. William Bocher, of Gainsforde, 1 May.
Alyce Bosall, 13 Maye.
ffrancis, s. Henrie Snellocke, 28 Maye.
Margaret, d. William Harrington, 7 June.
William Harrington, 24 June.
Rose Cant, widdow, 14 Julie.
Alyce, w. William Edward, of ffullers, 11 August.
Margaret Hart, widow, 3 October.
Zacharias Smith, alias Annis, 26 December.
Denis, w. Henrie Snellocke, 5 Januarie.
[88] Marian Edward, widow, 18 Januarie.
Joane Edward, widow, 16 March.
1599 A childe of Thomas Howe (unbaptized) the last day of April.
Joane Bayly, a poore girle that dwelt in this towyne, 11 May.
Joane Bayly, w. John Bayly, 6 Julie.
Samuel, s. Edward Ostler, 12 July.
Elizabeth, d. Robert ——,* 26 July.
Susanna, d. Thomas Harvey, 22 August.†
1600 Mary, d. Jonas Spiltimber, 14 June.
John ffisher, 18 June.
Elizabeth, w. Henry Smith, 23 Julye.
Henry, s. William Cracherod, 24 Julye.
Sara, d. William Edwards, younger, 23 August.
Rose, d. Richard Edwards, 10 Septembe.
Hercules, s. widow ffisher, 29 Septembe.
Ellenor Cornell, widow, 30 October.
Steven, s. Steven Cant, 12 ffebruarie.
1601 John Bragg, 21 March.
Mary, d. widdow Fisher, 15 November.
1602 Richard Pollard, 28 April.
Mother Kempe, an aged woman, 24 July.

---

*Name not clear; it may be Cozan.

†Down to this point the register has been copied by the same hand as the baptisms down to this date; the next eight entries are in the same hand as the baptisms of 1600; the original hand-writing occurs again in the entries for 1601-4, but evidently making original entries and not a copy as the ink varies much in color.

Ann, d. Mr. Jonson, of Habridg, 2 August.
Mathew Thorogood, 2 November.
Henry Cirke, 20 November.
Mary Buttoll, 19 December.
Widdow Harrington, an ancient woman, 3 ffebruary.
Mother Linwood, 8 ffebruary.

1603 William Buttolph, 12 Aprill.
Isaac Hart, 22 May.
Henry Read, a child, 27 May.
Mary Read, 2 June.
John Bunting, 16 July.
Clement Boreham, 2 October.
John, s. Richard Edward, 9 October.

1604 Mother Bush, 23 August.
Mother Stapleton, 2 August.
[89] John, s. Richd. Edwarde, 5 October.
Symon Grene, 1 January.
Alse, d. William Batten, 19 March.

1605 Jone, w. Thomas Browne, senior, 27 June.
Ann Pettit, an ancient woman, over 100 years ould, 7 October.
Samuel, s. Robert Devorax, 10 December.
Margere, w. John Pollard, 22 December.
Ould Mother Seaman, 6 ffebruary.
Margaret, w. Thomas Hurrell, 9 ffebruary.
John Read, the elder, 21 ffebruary.

1606 John Baley, 29 April.
Mary, w. Jonas Spiltimber, 13 May.
Ould Mother Hedg, 11 September.
Alse, d. William Batte, 21 October.
Margaret, d. Henry Petite, 14 January.
Dorothye, d. Richard Edwardes, January 18.

1607 Mary, wiefe of John Brande, September 15.
Mother Gipps, Januar 12.
Thomas Browne, senior, february 28.
Susan, wiefe of Mr. John Cracherode, february 11.
William Smitten, March 11.

1608 Mary, d. Thomas Cooke, April 11.
Mary, wiefe of Stephen Cannte, April 24.
John Hedge, an old man, June 19.

Mary, wiefe of Thomas Bayly, May —.
Michael Richardson, June 26.
1609 Roberte, s. John Pollard, June 30.
William Caunte, July 2.
Joan, w. John Clerke, February 9.
Mary, w. Lawrence More, 22 March.
Thomas, s. Thomas Chatterton, 23 March.
1610 Thomas, s. Henry Laver, 4 Aprill.
Richard, s. Hercules Evans, 12 Aprill.
Ann Butcher, an ould woman, 20 July.
Dorathy, d. Thomas Brown, 2 August.
Richard Everase, 21 August.
Joan Barber, an ould woman, 21 August.
William, s. James Shull, 23 September.
Robert Georg, 24 October.
Anne Kemp, 11 November.
Abraham Humpye, 4 December.
Ann, d. Clement Boreham, 19 January.
1611 John Read, of the hill, 22 June.
ffrancis, w. Thomas Plumb, 1 September.
1612 William Edward, sen., 22 March.
Thomas ffitch, 23 May.
Dorathye, w. William Butcher, 12 June.
Thomas, s. Thomas Browne, 23 Julie.
Margaret, d. Lowrance Moore, Jan. 18.
Henry Snellocke, Jan. 28.
John Pollerd, March 22.
1613 John Parker, Aprill 2.
Widdowe Cirke, April 20.
Rose, w. Richard Edwards, May 16.
Henry Smith, the elder, May 18.
William Massy, Aug. 18.
Thomas, s. John Perry, Nov. 21.
Susan, d. William Werhead, Jan. —.
Samuel, s. William Edward, Feb. —.
1614
[90] April 7. Anne, d. Richard Bucher.
April 18. Rebecca, d. Daniell Dod.
May 9. Robert Perry.
May 20. John Heart.

July 29. Joane Smitten.
Sept. 19. Oliver Stebben.
November 27. Elizabeth, w. Jerimie Pearman.
March 16. Ede, the base daughter of Adwy Fisher.
March 4. Phillis Pollard, widdowe.

1615 June 13. Hennery Cant.
July 24. Hennery, s. Hennery Pettit.
Sept. 3. Alice, w. William Read, the elder.
Sept. 12. Robert, s. John Browne.
Sept. 24. Rose Bacon, single woman.
Sept. 29. Adwy ffisher, single woman.
Dec. 7. Joice Spiltimber, single woman.

1616 May 9. Sarah, d. Josias Pollard.
May 11. Alice Harrington.
May 14. John Cousin.
July 21. Ellen, d. Jeames Shedd.
June 12. Anne, d. William Sparke.
Aug. 3. Joane ffytch, widow.
Aug. 18. Mathew, s. Hennery Bevis.
Sept. 9. ffrances, w. William Edwards, jun.
Nov. 27. Henry Smith.
December 26. Thomas Gardiner, the elder.
January 1. Thomas Edwards, of Bradfields.
January 25. Susanna, d. Richard Gippes.
March 2. Elizabeth, d. Giles Elsing.
March 2. Thomas, s. Richard Raven.

1617 March 28. Alse, d. Richard Raven.
May 10. Ellen Fisher.
Oct. 26. John, s. John Smythe.
Dec. 23. The wife of Hercules Evans.
Dec. 27. George Rule.
Jan. 8. Mary, w. Robert Edwards, the elder.
Jan. 23. William, s. Henry Bayley.
Jan. 28. Rebecca, d. Daniell Dod.
Feb. 1. Robert Warner, the elder.
Feb. 28. Jeremie Amie, of Abingen in Cambridge- [shire.
March 7. William, s. ——— Wallis.*
March 23. William Paine.

---

*Illegible; all the writing here is very bad, the letters not being carefully formed.

REGISTER. — BURIALS.

1618 June 14. Thomas Cracherode, gent., the elder.
Aug. 3. John, s. Thomas Mathew, alias Miche.
Sept. 4. Elizabeth, w. Thomas Harvy.
Nov. 3. Thomas, s. John [Gore ?].
Jan. 30. John Lampson, son-in-law to David Plaile.
February 2. Marie Buttall.
Feb. 25. William Read, senior.
[91] March 1. Roger Hayward.
March 19. Joane, w. Samuell Hamond.
March 23. Marie, w. Roger Edwards.
1619 March 31. Richard, s. Thomas Wight.
Aug. 20. Margaret, w. John Bust.
Nov. 28. Anne Bayly.
Feb. 9. Joane Rule, widdow.
1620 May 12. Ellen, w. John Cratchrode, gent.
July 9. Richard, s. Richard Read.
July 10. Alse, w. Edward Moore.
July 11. Daniel Dod.
July 17. Robert, s. William Read.
July 20. Alse, d. William Bateman.
Aug. 9. Henry Bevis.
Aug. 22. Mathew Bateman.
Sept. 1. William, s. William Spark.
Sept. 1. Tomazin, w. John Knoxs.
Sept. 3. Sara, d. William Boram.
Oct. 28. Robert Harrington.
Novemb. 24. John, s. John Ridgewell.
Dec. 4. Widdow Harrington, sen.
Dec. 29. Robert Pratt.
Feb. 6. Anne Gardiner.
Feb. 18. Henry Lidmore.
Feb. 25. Anne Evered, wid.
March 7. Edward Moore.
March 14. Saunder Buckley. [this place.
1621 April 20. Richard King, Dr. of Divinity & Rector of
John Cratcherood, gent., 6 July.
Amy, w. Jeremy Parmenter, 19 August.
Margaret, d. Adler Newman, 20 September.
Joanne ffinch, 19 November.
Ambrose Thompson, 10 December.

1622 Thomasin, w. Jeremy Pearmaine, 10 May.
[92] Mary, w. John Buckly, 26 May.
ffrancis, w. Samuel Edwards, 7 June.
Elizabeth, w. Richard Bateman, 2 July.
Joseph Marriner, 18 Sept.
John, s. John Drury, 7 November.
William, s. Joseph Marriner, 22 December.
[Samuel ?] s. Richard Edward, 9 March.*
1623 Tamosin, d. Jeremy Pearmaine, 19 June.
John Read, 23 June.
Mary Claidon, 23 July.
Susan, d. John Redgwell, 4 August.
Samuell, s. Samuell Symons, 4 November.
William, s. William ffitch, 28 November.
Jane, d. William Pamplin, 23 January.
Margaret Read, widdow, 10 March.
1624 Susan Mantt, 9 May.
Allice Batty, widdow, 3 June.
Allice, w. John Start.
Margarett Borum, widdow, 28 June.
William Simpson, 13 August.
Daniell, s. John Dod, 21 September.
Anne Hornsie, 5 October.
Robert Warner, 15 October.
Edward Ostler, 24 October.
Elizabeth Poole, 14 December.
[93] Samuell Smith, 5 March.
William Cracherode, gent., 10 March.
1625 William, s. Thomas Buttoll, 23 Aprill.
Ellenor Harvy, 15 May.
Richard Butcher, 24 June.
Agnes, w. Robt. Wankfourd, 4 July.
Agnes, d. Robt. Wankfourd, 19 August.
Allice, w. William Reade, 24 August.
Brigett, w. John ffisher, 27 August.
Mary, w. Thomas Greene, 8 September.
Thomas Chadderton, 15 September.
Joane, w. John Starte, 28 September.

*Partly erased, it is a baptism; there have been entries made and erased so as to be illegible down to the bottom of this page.

Mary, d. Raph Sewell, 5 October.
Thomas Baily, 24 October.
Elizabeth, w. William Bryant, 27 October.
Anne Butcher, 27 November.
Margaret South, 30 November.
Allice Evans, 30 December.
John Redgwell, 24 January.
Elizabeth, d. William Batty, 21 ffebruary.
Mary, w. Henry Paine, 25 ffebruary.

1626 William ffarrar, 25 March.
Thomas, s. William Levet, 25 March.
Roger Edwards, 26 March.
Sarah, w. Thomas Gardner, 4 Aprill.
Margarett Greene, widdow, 2 May.
Thomas, s. Robert Pollard, 21 May.

[94] John Bryant, the elder, 12 June.
William Johnson, 1 July.
Marie Allen, 5 August.
Anne, d. Thomas Trapnell.
Margarett, w. Henrie Clark, 5 August.
George, s. George Gyps, 18 August.
William, s. Roger Hoyden, 2 September.
Margarett Read, widdowe, 9 October.
Robert Edwards, the elder, 24 October.
Allice, w. Richard Paine, 30 October.
Susan, w. John Mising, 1 November.
Susan, d. Michael Richardson, 4 December.
Henrie, s. Henrie Paine, 29 December.
Thomasin ffuller, 29 January.
Grace, d. John Pollard, 7 March.
John, s. John Purchas, 18 March.   [2 Aprill.

1627 A wandering beggarman whose name was unknown,
Susan Cooke, 9 Aprill.
Rose, w. John ffisher, 15 Aprill.
Thomas, s. John Dod, 19 May.
Susan, d. Thomas Paynell, 28 June.
Thomas, s. William Bryant, 6 July.
Robert Edwards, of Comans, 19 July.
William, s. John Start, 24 August.
Robert, s. John Perrie, 6 September.

Joseph Bragg, 2 October.
Thomas, the base son of Marie Butcher, 27 October.
William Smith, of Graies, 22 November.
Thomas Mathew, 11 December.
Margerie, d. John Start, 12 December.
Allice, w. Richard Raven, 20 December.

[95] Susan, d. Rafe Sewell, 31 December.
Henrie Paine, 10 Januarie.
Grace, d. Widdow Battie, 15 March.
Judith, d. Henrie Bailie, 16 March.

1628 Joane, d. ffrancis Kendall, 24 June.
Marie, d. Robert Edwardes, the elder, 25 June.
John Start, the elder, 26 June.
Agnes, d. ffrancis Kandall, 19 Julie.
Robert, s. Ralfe Sewell, 19 Julie.
Henry Browne, 3 August.
Rafe, s. Rafe Sewell, 23 August.
Susan, w. William Levett, 16 September.
Rachell, w. John Gyps, the elder, 7 November.
Anne, w. John Mising, 7 November.
Elizabeth, d. Thomas Trapnell, 8 November.
Marie, w. Rafe Sewell, 8 Januarie.
William, s. John Perrie, 14 Januarie.
Daniell, s. John Busie, 12 ffebruary.

1629 Henrie Bailie, 10 Aprill.
Richard Paine, 28 May.
Marie, w. William Chadderton, 24 June.
John, s. John Drury, 23 August.
Thomas, s. Thomas Harvie, 2 October.
Marie, d. Roger Hoyden, 23 October.
Robert Hog, 29 December.
John Bryant, 29 January.
Anne, w. John Bellowes, 10 ffebruarie.
Sarah, w. Josias Pollard, 6 March.

1630
[96] ffrancis, d. Edward Clay, 16 Aprill.
Samuel, s. William Edward, of ffullers, 1 May.
Robert Siblie, 13 May.
Jone Bull, 26 May.
Marie, d. John Laver, 7 June.

REGISTER. — BURIALS. 63

Anne, d. Edward Clay, 26 June.
Elizabeth, d. Thomas Harvie, 3 July.
Anne, d. John Busie, 5 July.
Margarett, d. Edward Clay, 29 July.
Anne Harvy, 30 July.
Robert, s. Samuell Symons, 2 September.
John Buckly, 1 October.
Jone Ellis, 12 October.
Allice, w. —— Edward, of ffullers, 9 November.
Sarah, d. Steven Warner, 10 November.
David Warner, the elder, 11 Januarie.
Daniell, s. Barnard Sibly, 23 January.
Luce Houchin, widdow, 6 ffebruary.
Adler Newman, 15 ffebruary.
William, s. Thomas Emsden, 16 ffebruary.
Thomas Browne, 27 ffebruary.
Marie, d. Robert Ellis, 23 May.

1631 Margerie Titterell, 27 May.
John Bust, 7 August.
Arthur Winterfloud, 9 August.
Richard, s. Peter Hale, 22 August.
John Amys, 11 September.

[97] Rose, w. John Perrie, 14 September.
Agnes Smith, 5 October.
John, s. John ffitches, the younger, 16 October.
Alice Newman, 22 October.
Susan, d. John Bellowes, 12 November.
ffrancis, d. John Busie, 14 November.
Richard Paine, 20 December.
William Cosin, 25 January.
Philip Poole, 10 ffebruary.
Marie, w. Samuell Bateman, 17 ffebruary.
ffrancis, d. Samuell Edwards, of ffullers, 29 ffebruary.
Elizabeth Cosin, 7 March.

1632 William, s. Samuell Edwards, 30 April.
Elizabeth Spurge, 25 May.
William Greene, the elder, 27 June.
Samuell Bell, 8 July.
Anne, w. William Butcher, 3 August.
Marie, d. John Bryant, 10 August.

Thomasin Bailie, 16 August.
Rachell, w. William Edwards, of ffullers, 15 October.
Margarett Farrar, widdow, 20 October.
[98] Susan, w. John Gyps, the elder, 25 ffebruary.
1633 Hester, d. Robert Warner, 11 June.
Steven Cant, 10 July.
1634 Susan King, 8 June.
Roger Symons, 10 June.
Anna, d. Anna Scooline, 26 August.
Elizabeth Titterell, 19 September.
George Trapnell, 28 September.
Margaret Beard, 7 October.
Peter Argent, 16 November.
Henrie Bateman, 21 November.
Anne Symons, 27 November.
Anne Titterell, 28 November.
Marie Redgwell, 8 ffebruary.
Henrie Pettitt, the elder, 12 ffebruary.
Dorothy, w. Edmund Cocksedge, 12 ffebruary.
1635 William Pamplin, 18 Aprill.
Richard Titterell, 26 July.
Thomas Read, 16 August.
Lydia Edwards, 4 September.
[99] Lydia Wade, 23 September.
William Edwards, 25 September.
Thomas Browne, 3 October.
Peter Coote, 12 November.
Marie Paul, 4 December.
Anne Smith, widdow, 11 ffebruary.
Marie, w. Nathanaell Paul, 25 ffebruary.
1636 Elizabeth Perrie, widdow, 29 August.
William Bryant, 16 June.
Susan, w. Mr. Thomas Cracherode, 22 June.
Dorothy, w. Mr. Samuel Simons, 3 August.
John Southy, 18 August. [ber.
William, s. Robert Edwards, the younger, 18 Septem-
Grace Ostler, widdow, 20 September.
Sara Pamplyn, widow, 25 September.
Anne Cirke, a child, 19 October.
Anne, d. William Berd, a child, 5 November.

REGISTER. — BURIALS. 65

        Dorcas, d. John Laver & Mary, his wife, the last day of ffebruary.
        Susan, d. Thomas Harvey & Susan, 7 March.
        Mary ffisher, widow, 9 March.
        John Gyps, widower, 12 March.
        Samuel, s. Thomas Emsden & Elizabeth, 12 March.
1637 Robert Maltiward, s. Robert Maltiward, gent., 14 April.
[100] Susan Pettit, widow, 29 May.
        Elizabeth, d. Michael Richardson, 24 June.
        Elizabeth Monke, widow, 29 June.
        Barbara Laver, w. Henry Laver, 26 August.
        Joane ffinch, w. John ffinche, 10 September.
        Thomas Warner, 30 October.
        Clemence Clerke, w. Henry Clerke, 3 November.
        John, s. William Murken & ffrancis, 4 November.
        Judah Brewster, w. Robert Brewster, 13 December.
           [Robt. written and erased, Judah written over.]
        Hercules Eveins, 25 December.
        Alice ffitches, w. John ffitches, 27 December.
        Mary Mumford, w. John Mumford, 14 January.
        Jeremy Pareman, 14 February.
        ffrancis Simson, s. John Simson, 24 Jan.
        Rose Cooke, d. William Cooke, 29 January.
        Henery Clerke, widower, 6 Feb.
        The widow Bryant, 12 March.
1638 William, s. Edward Clay & Anne, 7 April.
        Alice Cosin, widow, 7 June.
        Katherine Chaterton, w. William Chaterton, 26 July.
        Elizabeth Earle, w. George Earle, 26 July.
        Allice* [?] w. John Perry.
        Thomas Harvy, 19 Aug.
        Mary South, 24 Aug.
        Mary, w. John Reade, 15 Sept.
        Margaret, d. Robert Pillow, 17 Sept.
        Susan, w. John Gipps, 5 October.
        Old More, 18 November.
        William, s. Edward Taylor & Elizabeth, 20 December.
        Dorothy, w. William Browne, 26 June.
        William, s. William Redgewell and Joane, 9 feb.

---

*Name written over an erasure and almost illegible.

Anne Edwards, w. William Edwards, 21 february.
1639 John Chambers, a child, 14 April.
John, s. John Bryant, 6 June.
Mary, d. William Browne, 10 June.
Anne Bowyer, 29 June.
George Earles, s. George Earles, 4 July.
Sarah, w. Henery Pettit, 15 July.
John Bowtell, 20 July.
Samuell, s. Samuell Bateman, 22 July.
[101] Thomas, s. Thomas Emsden, 25 July.
Thomas Mumford, 28 July.
Sarah, d. Henry Pettit, 18 August.
Elizabeth Edwards, widow, 19 August.
Robert Edwards, s. Richard Edwards, 21 August.
Alice, w. Robert Edwards, senior, 1 September.
John, s. William Reade, October 20.
Susan Newman, widow, October 24.
William, s. William Berd & Sarah, Oct. 30.
Elizabeth More, widdow, Nov. 12.
Christian Overed, w. John Overed, clerke, Nov. 20.
—— Amye, widdow.
Jonathan, s. Thomas Roote & Anne.
Sarah, w. William How, Jan. 12.
Martha, d. Michael Richardson, 8 March.
John Quie, the same day.
Thomas Edwards, March 10.
Robert, s. John Laver & Mary, was buryed March 15.
ffrancis Gall.
1640 Joane, w. William Redgewell, April 4.
David Warner, April 6.
William, s. William Redgewell & Joane, April 20.
Judah Pollerd, June 17.
Anne Busye, w. John Busye, June 21.
Anne, baseborn child of Anne Winterflood, June 28.
Anne, w. Thomas Warner, July 25.
Ellen, w. Robert Pollerd, Sept. 12.
Robert Harrington, gent., Sept. 27.
Elizabeth, d. Edward Tayler, Novemb. 28.
Robert Pollard, January 14.
——, s. Robert Pollard, feb. 1.

————— Warner, widow, feb. 22.
1641 Michael Richardson, the last day of May.
Susan, w. Sydney Eivens, June 11.
Margerie, w. William Boreham, June 21.
—————, d. Robert Warner, Sept. —.
ffrancis, d. John Briant, Nov. 24.
Henery Laver, the elder, December 7.
William Butcher, Dec. 14th.

This page is filled for nearly all of its length; it is followed by a page completely blank; the next page is dated 1655.

NOTE by the copyist.—Names found in this register which yet are borne by present (1902) inhabitants of Toppesfield and neighbourhood.

Allen (Alwin), Argent, Barber, Brewster, Bromley, Butcher, Clarke, Coote, Earl, Ellis, Fitch, Gurteen (Gurton), Hale, Hall, Houchin, Mumford, Newman, Pannell (Paynell), Parmenter, Purkis, Read, Ridgewell, Ruggles, Seaman, Shed, Smith, Sparrow, Wade, Yeldham. There were also Eleys here till quite recently.

There are houses called: Thurstons, Flowers Hall, Quays, Peacocks, Mortimers, Hurrells, probably after people named in these lists.

AN ELEGY ON THE
DEATH OF BENJAMIN KIMBALL, OF TOPSFIELD,
WHO DIED AUG. 19, 1775.

BY REV. JOHN CLEAVELAND.

Benjamin Kimball was the son of Jacob and Priscilla (Smith) Kimball of Topsfield. His father was a blacksmith and was possessed of musical talent. Jacob, another son of Jacob Kimball, was a drummer in the Revolution when only fourteen years of age and afterwards was a lawyer, teacher, and famous composer of music. Benjamin Kimball was born at Topsfield in 1757 (baptized, Aug. 21, 1757) and died Aug. 19, 1775. As a private he marched to Lexington in Capt. Joseph Gould's Company, and the following month he enlisted in Capt. Baker's Company as corporal, serving until Aug. 5, 1775. He died at his father's home in Topsfield. The house yet stands on Main street and of late years has been known as the Wildes-Hutchings house. The stone that marks his grave, in what is now the Pine Grove Cemetery, bears the following inscription:

"In memory of Mr. Benjami^n Kimball, late Student of Harvard College; who, after a Distressing Illness which he bore with that chearfull Resignation, which characterizes tho^{s}ₑ Whose Religion is of the heart, Died, Augt 19th 1775, Æt. 19.

    Tho' Sin's illusive joys awhile may Charm
    Mankind, they lead to endless Woe & Death.
    But Virtue, rich & Steadfast Blessings yields;
    Support thro' Life & Wings the Soul for Heaven."

ELEGY ON DEATH OF BENJAMIN KIMBALL. 69

In the *Essex Gazette*, of Sept. 7, 1775, appears the following obituary notice:

"Last Saturday Evening died at Topsfield, Mr. Benjamin Kimball late student at Harvard College, Son of Mr. Jacob Kimball of that Town. His Illness was a Fever and Dysentery in which he was exercised with great Pain, which he sustained with great Patience and remarkable submission to the Divine Will. His Hopes of eternal life were firm and strong to the very last which enabled him to entertain the Views of his Dissolution with a Calmness and Serenity of Mind which was truly surprising, as well as satisfying and comforting to all who conversed with him in his sickness."

The following elegy was written by the Rev. John Cleaveland, pastor of a church at Chebacco Parish in Ipswich, now the town of Essex. The original manuscript is preserved in the Cleaveland MSS. at the Essex Institute, Vol. I, page 63. The Rev. John Cleaveland is well known for his controversial writings with Dr. Mayhew and others. He was Chaplain of a regiment in Gen. Abercombie's expedition against Canada in 1758 and the following year he was Chaplain in the campaign against Louisburg. His son, Nehemiah, studied medicine with Dr. Manning, of Ipswich, and afterwards settled at Topsfield, where he passed a long life of distinguished usefulness.

An Elegy on the Death of M[r] Benj[a] Kimball, Late Student of Harvard Colledge, Who Departed this Life, August the 19, 1775, in the 19th year of his Age.

1

Ah! dear deceased Friend,
No more with the
A useful hour I spend
In Colloquy;
Nor more thy Face behold,
Nor hear thy lips unfold
The Worthy thoughts enrolled
Within thy Breast.

2

But tho thy Body dead
Is urn'd in dust,
Thy vivid soul has fled
To find I trust,
From every sin and Woe,
Which with the Body Grow,
And vex us here below,
A Refuge Safe.

3

The Fears of Death which haunt,
And here molest
Thy Brethren Saints whome want
Thy perfect Rest,
From the have bore their Wing.
Ah, Death has lost his sting!
Now VICI thou shall Sing
For ever more.

4

This thou didst clearly see,
O Spirit blest,
While thou this House of Clay
As yet possest.
When by thy Sickness pain'd,
When wrapt in Joys unfeigned
And not to be explained
By mortal tongue,

5

Undaunted thou didst cry,
"O Death what Sting!
"O grave what Victory!
"You with you Bring?
"How can I here Remain,
"Where Sin and Sorrow rein
"No more kind Death, refrain
"To seize my Breath.

6

"My Friends, you are to me
"Most near and Dear:
"Mourn not for me, I Pray;
"But let the Tear
"Which from your Eyes now flows
"Be freely shed for those
"Whom living Sins and Woes
"Ever await.

7

"But though I value so,
"My Kindred dear,
"Death's changes too, I know,
"Most awfull are.
"Tis yet my chief Request
"By Dying to be blest.
"Where Does my God exist?
"O, there's my Heaven."

8

Thus with chearfull look,
And Heart Resign'd
This more than conqirer spoke,
Who much inclined
For every Creatures Weal,
Was fir'd with warmest Zeal
To save from endless Hell
Immortal Souls.

9

Rejoice ye Born of Heaven,
And let you Praise
To JESUS Free be given:
For think this grace
Clusters spie has found
In Canans promis'd Ground,
And left to chear your bound
To the same Rest.

10

Thy love and Zeal for Truth*
Were shewn, O Saint
When with Apollo's youth
Thou didst Frequent,
With glad and chearfull Heart,
Our Harverell's Seat of Art
To share the Noblest part
Of Joys terrene.

11

Now I concieve thy thought
Of Truth has gain'd
What it Had vainly Sought,
If here detain'd,
In constant clost essay,
Till Fourscore years Decay:
So more and more for Aye
Thy Wisdom Grows.

12

Thus Want of wisdom's light
Shall be Supply'd:
Naught more of error's night
Shall the betide;
But in eternal Day,
Where pure Scientia's Ray
Can naught but truth convey,
Shall thou Reside.

13

These Hopes, which the did Bless,
Must not be Sold
For Worlds transformed to Mass
Of Purest Gold,
(Nay more) they're not bestow'd
For Prayers or Tears of Blood,
Or Acts of Moral Good
There price to mean;

---

*Learning.

14

But these so precious Gems
On Calverys Hill
Were bought for crimson streams
Which there did spill
Free from the Buyer's vein,
To give to those of Men
Who faintless ne'er restrain
Their ardent Prayers.

15

Dear Friend, Death soon shall sieze
Likewise on me:
O may I Reach thy Bliss
And Joine with thee,
And all the holy throng
To Praise in endless Song
Him who from endless wroung,
Sinners redeemed.

SMITH FAMILY LETTERS.

The following letters were printed in the *Deseret Evening News*, published at Salt Lake City, Utah, in the year 1872, George A. Smith, President of the Church of Jesus Christ of Latter-Day Saints, having found the original letters in the possession of J. Perkins Towne, for many years town clerk of Topsfield. For some account of Asael and Samuel Smith, see Topsfield Historical Collections, Vol. VIII, pages 87-101.

"Tunbridge, Jan. 14th, 1796.

"*Respected Sir.*—Having a favorable opportunity, altho' on very short notice, I with joy and gratitude embrace it, returning herewith my most hearty thanks for your respect shown in your favor of the 30th of November, by Mr. Willes, which I view as a singular specimen of friendship, which has very little been practiced by any of my friends in Topsfield, altho' often requested.

"My family are all, through the goodness of the Divine Benediction, in a tolerable good state of health, and desire to be remembered to you and to all inquiring friends.

"I have set me up a new house since Mr. Willes was here, and expect to remove into it next spring, and to begin again on an entire new farm, and my son Joseph will live on the old farm (if this that has been but four years occupied can be called old), and carry it on at the halves, which half I hope will nearly furnish my family with food, whilst I with my four youngest sons shall endeavor to bring to another farm, etc.

"As to news, I have nothing, as I know of, worth noticing, except that grain has taken a sudden rise amongst us, about one-third.

"As to the Jacobin party, they are not very numerous here, or if they are they are pretty still; there are some in this State, viz., in Bennington, who, like other children crying for a rattle, have blared out against their rulers, in hopes to wrest from them, if possible, what they esteem the plaything of power and trust. But they have been pretty well whipt and have become tolerably quiet again, and I am in hopes, if they live to arrive to the years of discretion, when the empire of reason shall take place, that they will then become good members of society, notwithstanding their noisy, nucious behavior in their childhood, for which they were neither capable of hearing or giving any reason.

"For my part, I am so willing to trust the government of the world in the hands of the Supreme Ruler of universal nature, that I do not at present wish to try to wrest it out of his hands, and I have so much confidence in his abilities to teach our Senators wisdom, that I do not think it worth while for me to interpose, from the little stock of knowledge that he has favored me with, in the affair, either one way or the other. He has conducted us through a glorious revolution and has brought us into the promised land of peace and liberty, and I believe that he is about to bring all the world into the same beatitude in his own time and way; which, altho' his ways may appear never so inconsistent to our blind reason, yet may be perfectly consistent with his designs. And I believe that the stone is now cut out of the mountain without hands, spoken of by Daniel, and has smitten the image upon his feet, by which the iron, the clay, the brass, the silver, and the gold (viz.,), all the monarchial and ecclesiastical tyranny will be broken to pieces and become as the chaff of the summer thrashing floor, the wind shall carry them all away, that there shall be no place found for them.

"Give my best regards to your parents and tell them that I have taken up with the Eleventh commandment, that the negro taught to the minister, which was thus—

"The minister asked the negro how many commandments there were, his answer was, 'Eleben, sir.' 'Aye,' replied the other, 'what is the Eleventh? that is one I never heard of.' 'The Elebenth commandment, sir, is mind your own business.'

"So I choose to do, and give myself but little concern about what passes in the political world.

"Give my best regards to Dr. Meriam, Mr. Willes, Joseph Dorman, and Mr. Cree, and tell Mr. Cree I thank him for his respects and hope he will accept of mine. Write to me as often and as large as you can and oblige your sincere friend and well wisher,"

ASAEL SMITH.

"MR JACOB TOWN, JUN."

The following appears on the back of the first page of the letter, being evidently of the nature of a postcript—

"Give my hearty thanks to Mr. Charles Rogers for his respect shown in writing me a few lines, and tell him that I should a wrote to him now had I had time, but now waive it for the present, as I have considerable part of what I intended to a writ to you.

"If I should live and do well, I expect to come to Topsfield myself next winter, which, if I do, I shall come and pay you a visit. Farewell.

"Tell Mr. Joseph Cree that if he will come here and set up his trade, I will warrant him as much work as he can do, and good pay."

On the margin of the second page of the letter appears the following—

"I expect my son Joseph will be married in a few days."

On the outside of the letter, besides the superscription, "Mr Jacob Town, Topsfield, Commonwealth of Massachusetts," is this, "Rec'd. Feb. 14, 1796, from Asael Smith."

From which it appears that the letter was one month on the journey from Tunbridge, Vt., to Topsfield, a distance of 150 miles, and was probably carried by a private conveyance.

The letter amounts almost to a prophecy, and manifests the strong faith of the writer in the stability and permanence of the then new government of the United States, under the over-ruling hand of the Almighty.

BOSTON, Feb. 2nd, 1782.

"*Sir*—I have taken this opportunity to write to you to let you know that it is trying times here. The prices of our clothing are much cut down—linen shirts are put at 10s, cotton and linen are put at 12s, shoes are put at 10s. The rest of our things they have allowed as we set them, but they have allowed 2-6-3 for collecting and transporting said articles. The muster roll we sent they liked very well, but the amount of supplying the soldier's families we must lose for aught anything I see, for the court have repealed all the laws respecting that matter, though many towns have done as we did, yet must lose it.

"I have taken the money for the clothing in the new paper money, as it is to be taken for rates in the treasury. I have sent ye money by Capt. Gould to you and desire you to deal it out where it ought to go if they want it before I come home. I don't know as I shall come home till near March. The new paper money will answer in ye treasury as well as silver, and if you can get any body to take ye paper to pay their rates, I should be glad if you would change it and pay Madame Emerson silver. I desire you to let my family know that I am well. I am in a great hurry. Mr. Perkins is going to Topsfield, so no more at present. I am your friend,"

SAMUEL SMITH.

"It being now ye 7 day."

REMINISCENCES OF REV. ASAHEL HUNTINGTON.

The following letter addressed to Richard Phillips of Topsfield, was written by Dr. Humphrey Gould of Rowe, Massachusetts. The original letter passed into the hands of the late Rev. James H. Fitts and in 1904 was presented by Mrs. Fitts to the Topsfield Historical Society.

December 14, 1869.

My Dear Sir,

You have settled or are about to settle a new minister over the Congregational Society of Topsfield, a society founded in part by my ancestors. My great-great-grandfather was an active and efficient member of the society and a member of the church and I very naturally take an interest in it. All my forefathers from Zaccheous Gould the 1st down were members. An Ecclesiastial History of the town would be very interesting for there are many curious facts if brought out in an attractive form would be pleasant [torn] prosperity and peace have not always escaped discord and strife. In Mr. Capen's day there were among the people political troubles which disturbed the peace of the church. My ancester Capt. John Gould was a high liberty man, he and a man by the name of Howe, I think took opposite sides in Politics, the worthy Capt. withdrew from the communion which was a source of grief to tender conciences, but when the causes of the strife were removed by the departure of Gov. Andros like wise and sensible men they agreed to bury the hatchet and live again in christian fellowship, and at a meeting of the church they shook hands and became reconciled to each other.

REMINISCENCES OF REV. ASAHEL HUNTINGTON.

My memory goes back many years, to the time of Mr. Huntington. There are some things connected with his settlement and history that are very interesting. He was settled I think in the year 1787. An ordination in those olden times was a very important event in the history of the town, the day of ordination was a great holiday, a day of great enjoyment not only to the people of the town but many of the neighboring towns. There was great feasting, preparation was made to entertain all who might attend. My father and mother were in the prime of life, living with their adopted father Zaccheus Gould a man of sterling worth and of large property. They entertained two hundred persons mainly from Middleton. When I was a boy I often heard a discription of that entertainment. There were some persons present by the name of Avery living near Middleton Bridge who were particularly distinguished as enormous eaters, even the very manner of their eating was described.

In that day there were few if any carriages. People generally rode on horses and there were a hundred horses turned into the pastures. You can judge by this somewhat of the number of people present on that joyous occasion. My great uncle as I have said was a man of worth, was esteemed a religious man was in fact a genuine Puritan a strict observer of the Sabbath and of course did not think much of amusements, but he yielded gracefully to the spirit of the occasion and gave up that great west room to the young people as a dancing hall, and they had music and dancing till morning perhaps.

There are pleasant memories connected with those old times, and the first people were often dignified in their manners though some times somewhat formal. Perhaps you would like to know how they treated their new minister and his bride when he brought her to her new home. A part of the people went to meet them and escort them into town while another portion repaired to the house to receive them upon their arrival. My father and mother were at the house. The ladies were dressed in their silks and satins, the gentlemen in their best attire. They made an opening the ladies on one side and the gentlemen on the other and the bridegroom and bride passed into the house. Mrs. Huntington was quite mortified as she had on only a common riding dress. Thus you see they were most courteously received and proved to be worthy of all the honors rendered them in the life they led among the people. Mr. Huntington's ministry was a most useful one. He was the minister of my youth. From his holy hands was administered the right of baptism, that beautiful ordinance now going into disuse, upon my innocent person and I received his blessing. How do I know but it was a blessing indeed. He was my school-master, under his instruction I began to commit to memory. He was a most genial man, greatly revered and beloved by the children. When he visited at my father's he went round and patted all the boys upon the head speaking pleasant words. How happy we all felt. To give an extended account of my recollections of Mr. H., as a preacher, a school-master and a citizen would require too much space for a letter. As a theologian he was a Calvinist, not an ultra but a moderate. We had two sermons upon the Sabbath, a sermon before communion, and at the meeting of the ministerial associations, but never any extra meetings. In that day it would have been deemed irregular and downright heretical to have had evening meetings so common now. The people and minister were perfectly united, lived in harmony and peace, and when this worthy man died there was universal mourning. Save old Henry Bradstreet. My hope is that your new minister will possess all the good qualities of the worthy man I loved so well. I trust he possesses fair talents, is well endowed with good learning, is a pious man but not a **pietest** and above all things will *keep* himself *aloof* from all *parties* and then he may be a useful man.

Excuse the freedom I have taken in writing this long letter.

And be assured I am truly,
       Yours,
        HUMPHREY GOULD.

R. PHILLIPS, ESQ.

LETTER FROM JOHN PEABODY, JR., IN 1811.

Topsfield, September 4th, 1811.

DEAR BROTHER—having been called upon this evening to watch with Mr. Barth^w Conant who is now sick with the dysentary; I have taken my pen & paper in order to fill up a leasure lonsome hour in writing a few lines to you who I hope are at this moment reposing your head on downy pillow in the quiet enjoyment of peaceful slumbers. I have the happiness to tell you that our Fathers family & mine are in usual health. God grant it may be continued. We have indications of a sickly time—several are now sick and since you left Topsfield two of its inhabitence have gone to give up their great account. The first was Mrs. Andrews consort of Mr. Joseph Andrews. While sitting in a chair she without complaining suddenly fell down and expired. Her age was 36 years. The other was Mr. Edward Hammond who died August 29th, aged 31 years. A few months ago he was (as you very well know) the picture of health and uprightness but now alas where is he? These are loud calls to us my Brother, and shall we not regard the voice of him that speaketh? Infinite grace grant that we may. I rejoice to hear that your health is somewhat better and soon I hope you will be able to say I am well, but as we are not to expeet mericles in this degenerate age I hope you will take wisdom for your counsellor & let prudence & temperance be ever your constant companion, and doubtless you will be richly benefitted by their society. I enclose 3 dollars with which you will please to purchase me (if you can find time) two quarter Tickets in the Dixville lottery. You will be careful to by at one of those lucky offices and then surely I must draw.

The rediculous conduct of the Govr & Councel and their satellites (mentioned in your last) would excite a horse laughf did not the dreadful consequence of such misrule which we now feel and the still more dreadful wich we apprehend to forcibly forbid it. On this subject I could expatiate with freedom, but as vastly abler pens are constantly employed upon it, and as your situation enables you to understand it more thoroughly any remarks of mine would be useless.

John Peabody J^r.*

A. B. Peabody.

N. B. Please to inform me if you know who are the new appointed officers. Any information respecting the views, feelings & intentions of Bostonians relating to the [   ] war with England, the new Bank, &c, &c, would be greatfully received.

J. P.

[Addressed to] M^r. A. B. Peabody,

Boston.

From Essex Institute MSS. Coll.

---

*John Peabody and Aaron B. Peabody were brothers of Joel R. Peabody and both were born in the house now occupied by Charles J. Peabody.

REVOLUTIONARY WAR RECORDS.

In Council, July 24th, 1776.

Ordered, that Leiutenant Thomas Murray, Ensign Nath[l] Fitzpatrick, & Cladius Charles Surgeon All persons taken and brought into Salem by the Colony Sloop Terrannicide, be upon signing the parole ordered by this Board, before Witnesses be removed from there to the Town of Topsfield in the County of Essex there to put under the Care of the Committee of Safety &c of said Town & to be confined within the limits Thereof and the Committee aforesaid are hereby Directed in all Respects to Conduct themselves, Respecting the Prisoners Aforesaid agreeable to the Resolve of the Continentell Congress and the Sheriff of the County of Essex or his Deputy are hereby ordered as soon as may be, to Conduct the prisoners aforesaid from Salem to Topsfield aforesaid & there to Deliver to the Committee of Safety of Said Town to be by them Dealt with as aforesaid.

Jn° Avery, Dep[y] Sect.

Mass. Archives, Vol. 65, page 467.

In a bill from the Selectmen of Gloucester to the Colony of Massachusetts Bay, dated Jan. 16, 1776, for items of expense incurred between Aug. 22 and Dec. 31, 1775, occurs the following item:

"To 3 cords of wood for 61 men from Topsfield, Boxford, and Rowley, to defend the Town against the threats of the enemys."

Mass. Archives, Vol. 180, page 288.

An Account of Donations received by Samuel Adams, Isaac Smith, and Thomas Russell, Esq., from the several Towns of the Commonwealth of Massachusetts by virtue of a brief of said Commonwealth for the suffering inhabitants of South Carolina and Georgia.

April 4, 1782, Topsfield. The Rev[d]. Mr. Daniel Breck, £7. 16. 0.

Mass. Archives, Vol. 158, page 481.

THE PEABODY–BATCHELDER–YOUNG HOUSE

ON NORTH STREET, TOPSFIELD.

BY JOHN H. TOWNE.

This two-story house was built for Lieut. Francis Peabody, the "Ancestor," a few years before his death which occurred Feb. 19, 1698. According to family tradition, and other sources of information, this house was erected in 1692, the year of the Witchcraft delusion, upon land that he purchased from William Symonds. No doubt the oak timber used was sawed out at his own saw-mill, which was built in 1672, and stood on the stream below. But this was not Francis Peabody's first habitation, for he came to Topsfield from Hampton, N. H., as early as 1657, and probably first settled near this site, or, where his other house stood by the grist-mill, and which was taken down in 1846. Lieut. Peabody was a very prominent man in town and church affairs, holding offices for many years. He was also one of the largest land owners in the town, holding at one time over fifteen hundred acres located in Topsfield, Boxford, and Rowley. At his death this house and farm came into the possession of his son Isaac Peabody, who, like his father, was a prominent man in the town, serving as selectman for a number of years, and as representative to the Legislature. The exact date of the death of Isaac is not known, but by will dated October 21, 1726, and which proved and allowed at a Probate Court, held at Ipswich, on January 2[d], 1727, he gave the buildings and two-thirds of the farm-lands to his son Isaac Peabody, jr. The other one-third of the farm-land was bequeathed to his son Joseph, together with the mills, and the dwelling-house nearby. Isaac, jr., owned the place and lived here until his death, which occurred Jan'y. 13, 1739, in the forty-second year of his age. Not leaving any direct heirs or disposing

THE PEABODY-BATCHELDER-YOUNG HOUSE.

From a photograph taken about 1875 and now in the possession of Augustus V. Peabody, of Malden, Mass. Benjamin P. Adams, Samuel S. McKenzie, and Nehemiah Cleaveland (from left to right) are standing before the house.

of his property by will, it went to his brothers and sisters. They sold the buildings and farm on May 21, 1739, for £558, to John Batchelder of Wenham, who married, Dec. 13, 1727, Anne Peabody, a sister of Isaac. By this transfer the place went out of the Peabody name, although to one of the heirs. John Batchelder died Feb. 2, 1771 and this property afterwards came into the possession of his son John Batchelder who married for his first wife, May 15, 1765, widow Lydia Chapman, by whom he had several children. After her death, he married for a second wife, Aug. 30, 1812, Mrs. Lydia, widow of Capt. Daniel Boardman, who survived him. He died here Jan. 10, 1819.

This place was owned by the Batchelder's over eighty-four years, and they and their descendants have been active in state and town affairs. The place was finally sold by Jacob Batchelder, son of John, to Aaron Kneeland, Sept. 20, 1823. During Aaron Kneeland's ownership, his sons, Humphrey and Aaron Porter, lived here, the latter for many years, and most of his children were born in this house. Aaron Kneeland sold the buildings and farm, June 19, 1852, to Capt. Lorrance W. Wiihr, of Salem. Capt. Wiihr was an old sea captain, sailing out of Salem on "East India" voyages for many years. He occupied the place about two years, and then returned to Salem, having sold the farm, May 4, 1854, to Samuel S. Williston of Salem, who occupied it only a few months and then returning to Salem, conveyed the property back to Capt. Wiihr, on Feb. 27, 1855, who rented the place for a time to Mrs. Sally G., widow of Cyrus Kneeland. Capt. Wiihr finally sold the farm, Apr. 18, 1857, to Mrs. Eliza Ricker, mother of the late George W. Ricker. She conveyed the property, Apr. 14, 1863, to Judith H., wife of George W. Ricker. It was during the ownership of the Ricker's that a new barn was built near what is now called North street, but it was afterwards moved to near the site of the old barn by the house. Methodist revival meetings were held in the evening in the west room of the house for nearly six months, during the years 1857-8, and many persons were converted. Mrs. Judith H. Ricker sold the property to Capt. Hiram P. Barker of Chelsea on Feb. 14, 1865.

Capt. Barker was a veteran of the Civil War and returned

in very poor health from which he never recovered. He died here Oct. 16, 1867. His heirs conveyed the estate, May 12, 1868, to Charles W. Burbank of Salem, store-keeper. During his ownership the farm was carried on by his wife's father, John C. Nye and others. Mr. Burbank did not live here much of the time, being at Salem in charge of his store. He died there on May 9, 1879, and his widow Louisa P. Burbank sold the property, on Apr. 9, 1881, to John Welch, who had been living in the house for some time.

John Welch died Apr. 20, 1882, and by his will dated Apr. 14, 1882, he bequeathed the buildings and land to his wife, Nettie L. Welch, who conveyed the property, June 20, 1885, to Isaac B. Young, the present owner. During his occupancy he has made several changes. The huge chimney was taken down in 1886 and new ones were built. The house was somewhat remodeled inside at the same time, and in 1891, a large addition was erected in the rear with a stable attached.

Although the old house at the first held within its oaken frame the Ancestor of all the Peabody's in America, and has now withstood the destroying elements of time for more than two centuries, yet it bids fair to be preserved for several other generations. Long may it stand in honor of those who here have lived and died.

THE BOYD-PEABODY-WATERS HOUSE

ON SALEM STREET, TOPSFIELD.

BY JOHN H. TOWNE.

This two-story house with long sloping roof, situated at the corner of Wenham and Salem streets, is supposed to have been built during the latter part of the 17th century. The house with other buildings, and seventeen acres of land, was owned and occupied for many years by Samuel Boyd.

THE BOYD-PEABODY-WATERS HOUSE
From a photograph taken in 1905.

Probably his five children were all born in this old house between the years 1720-1736. On the 30th of April, 1725, he bought three acres of land adjoining his farm, from David Comings, the son of John. On Sept. 30, 1736, Mr. Boyd conveyed the dwelling-house, outbuildings, and twenty acres of land for £360, to Matthew Peabody, son of Isaac, and the grandson of Lieut. Francis Peabody.

During the ownership of Matthew Peabody he increased the acreage of the farm and here he lived until his death which occurred October 20, 1777. Both he and his descendants have been prominent in town and church affairs. By will dated May 2d, 1774, Matthew Peabody gave to his son John Peabody, all his lands, with the buildings thereon, and the farm remained in John's possession until his death which occurred Jan. 29, 1802.

It seems by the records, that his real estate was not settled for several years, or until May 20, 1816, when an agreement was signed by his two sons, John, jr. and Ebenezer Peabody, dividing the same.

By agreement the farm on the hill, now owned by Charles J. Peabody, was conveyed to John Peabody, jr., and the old homestead formerly owned by Matthew, was conveyed to Ebenezer Peabody, who owned it until his death July 16, 1825, at the age of 46 years and 10 months.

On February 14, 1860, the old homestead came into the possession of Ephraim P. Peabody, one of the sons of Ebenezer, by the purchase of the interest of the remaining heirs.

On May 4, 1864, Ephraim P. Peabody sold the dwelling-house, carriage-house, and shed with twelve acres of land to James Waters, who owned it for several years, building a new barn in 1875. He lived here until his death Nov. 2d, 1885. The property was finally sold by his widow, Mary G. Waters, on April 23, 1889, to Alden P. Peabody, the present owner, and a descendant of Matthew Peabody.

A PATRIOTIC SONG.

SAID TO HAVE BEEN COMPOSED BY SETH PEABODY.*

(1) Old England, forty years ago,
　　When we were young and tender,
　She aimed at us a mortal blow,
　　But God was our Defender.

(2) She sent her fleets and armies forth,
　　To ravish, kill and plunder,
　Our heroes met them on the shore,
　　And beat them back like thunder.

(3) Decatur, Hull and Bainbridge dear,
　　Did wonders in our navy.
　Brave Captain Hull took the Guerriere,
　　And Bainbridge sank the Java.

(4) Decatur took a ship of fame,
　　High on the wavy water,
　The "Macedonia" was her name,
　　And home in triumph brought her.

(5) We had Green, Gates and Putnam,
　　To manage in the field.
　A gallant train of footmen,
　　Who would rather die than yield.

---

*Seth Peabody, son of Matthew Peabody, was born in Topsfield, Nov. 27, 1744, in the house described on the previous pages. He removed to Alfred, Maine, and was one of the six men who built, in 1766, the first saw-mill in the town. In 1771 he married Abigail Kimball and settled in Kennebunk, Maine. He served in the army during the whole Revolutionary War, and died at Canaan, Maine, in 1827, aged 83 years.

A PATRIOTIC SONG.

(6)   A stately troop of horsemen,
        Trained in a martial way,
    To augment our forces
        In North America.

(7)   Let William Hull be counted null,
        And let him not be named
    Upon the rolls of valient souls,
        Of him we are ashamed.

(8)   For his campaign was worse than vain,
        A coward and a traitor,
    For paltry gold his army sold
        To Brock, the speculator.

(9)   There were two mighty speakers
        Who ruled in Parliament,
    Who always had been seeking
        Some mischief to invent.

(10)   North, and Burke, his partner,
        A horrid plan did lay
    A mighty tax to gather
        In North America.

(11)   To subjugate us then we knew
        Was surely their design,
    For the laws they had enacted
        Were of the blackest kind.

(12)   Those cruel and oppressive laws
        They never would revoke,
    So we met them on the battle-field
        And severed the British yoke.

(13)   Then our independence they confessed,
        And with their hands they signed it,
    But on their hearts 'twas not impressed,
        For there we ne'er could find it.

(14) Now the Philadelphia Courier
　　　We want for information,
　　That we may well the right maintain
　　　Of our beloved nation.

(15) I am an old gray-headed man,
　　　My locks are white as cotton,
　　I fought the British and their aids,
　　　Till they were fairly beaten.

INSCRIPTIONS FROM

THE LAKE BURYING-GROUND.

David Lake | Died | June 26, 1842 | Aged 60 Yrs | & 9 mo.

Sarah, | wife of | David Lake | died Dec. 14, 1858 | Æt. 74 years.

David Lake Jr. | died at Sea | While on his Passage | to California | Apr. 28, 1859 | Æt. 52 yr's,

　　A kind and affectionate Husband and Father.

Hattie T. | wife of | David Lake | died Aug. 30, 1867 | Æt. 53 yrs. 8 mos. 14 d'ys. | Harriet E. Their infant daut. | died Oct. 19, 1836.

　　How shall I watch for thee when fears are stronger,
　　As night draws dark, and darker on the hill;
　　How shall I weep, when I can watch no longer,
　　Oh! art thou absent, art thou absent still,
　　　　Linger not longer.

Mrs. Anna | wife of | John B. Lake | Died | June 8, 1846 | Aged 33.

Mrs. Rebecca | Wife of | John B. Lake | who died | Aug. 12, 1843 | Aged 24.

FRANCIS PEABODY'S WILL, AND INVENTORY OF HIS ESTATE, 1698.

COPIED BY ANNIE F. TOWNE, A DESCENDANT.

The Last Will and Testament of Lieut. Francis Pebody of Topsfield in ^{ye} county of Essex in New-England: I Francis Pebody taking into consideration the uncertainty of my life & ^{ye} certainty of my Death being of perfect understanding & memory have seen good to make such a disposall of the temporall estate which God of his grace hath given me in this world as followeth—

Impr. I committ my immortall Soul into the hands of God & my body to a descent buriall when God shall take me out of this world.

Secundo. I give to my Son John Pebody & Joseph Pebody all that tract of Land which I bought of Merchant Joseph Jewitt of Rowley which Land lyeth in Boxford, I give to my Son John two thirds of ^{ye} aforesaid tract of Land & to my Son Joseph ^{ye} other third which I do give to them & to their Heirs forever & moreover I do give to them both in common currant pay (not money) five pounds to each of them, y^t is five pounds apiece besides what I have already given them.

Item. I do give to my Son William Pebody all that Land which I bought of John Tod Senr. of Rowly & of John Perley (excepting one hundred acres) which land I do give to him & to his Heirs forever, moreover I do give to him five pounds besides what he hath had of me already, which I do the rather on Consideration of his being (by ye providence of God) deprived of ^{ye} use of one of his arms, wch five pounds is to be paid as is above specified.

Item. I do give to my Son in Law Daniell Wood that hundred acres of Land which is above excepted to my Son William & is already in part possessed by my Son in Law Daniell Wood which said Land I do give to him & to his Heirs forever it being in Consideration of what I was obliged to do for him when come to age & provided y^t he shall be satisfied therewith on y^t account & give a discharge thereof to such of it shall concern which Land I have already promised & do purpose forthwith to make him a deed of in a way of firm conveyance in which Deed I shall bound & Limit ye aforesaid hundred acres accordingly.

Item. I do give to my Son Isaac Pebody all the land y^t I now live upon which I bought of M^r. Simons & my will is y^t my Son Isaac shall have all ye said Land which lyeth on ye South Side of ye brook running through the said farm both upland & meadow so bounded. I give my Son Isaac Pebody together wth my dwelling house & housing, orchard with Millyard wth all y^t I bought of William Evans & moreover I give to my Son Isaac from ye bridge all ye meadow downward on ye North East side of ye brook wch runneth through Tho. Doman's Meadow, as also I do give to my Son Isaac a Rod & half of upland adjoining to ye aforesaid meadow all along for ye bringing of his hay from time to time wch aforesaid Land I do give to my Son Isaac & his Heirs forever, together wth seventy acres of land on ye South side of ye River near to ye dwelling of Joseph Town Jun., Also I give to my son Isaac that bed with the furniture thereunto belonging which he now hath ye improvement of & this I would have noted, That I have given ye more to my son Isaac on consideration of ye providence of God dismatling him by ye loss of one of his Leggs.

Item. I do give to my Grandchild Jocob Pebody (ye son of my Son Jacob deceased) ye house which his father dwelt in together with all ye upland on ye side of ye brook y^t is on ye North side of ye abovesaid brook, as also all ye meadow on ye same side of ye brook from ye bridge & so upward, my will is y^t in Case my said Grandchild Jacob Pebody do live to ye age of twenty one years y^t then he shall have as is abovesaid to injoy himself & his Heirs forever. But in case ye said Jacob live not to y^t age then any of my other Sons shall have liberty to have ye land & house aforesaid provided y^t he or they shall pay to my grand-children Kezia & Mercy Pebody ye children of my Son Jacob deceased an hundred & twenty pounds in common currant pay (not silver.) Notwithstanding what is abovesaid in case ye said Jacob should have issue before he should arrive at ye aforesaid age y^t ye said Land shall be at ye disposal of ye abovesaid Jacob Pebody together wth ye house aforesaid. Also I do give to my grandchildren Kezia & Mercy Pebody ye children of my Son Jacob deceased I do give to each of them thirty acres of Land apiece provided that they shall live to ye age of eighteen years, which Threescore acres of Land Lyeth on ye south side of ye River in ye South West Division beyond M^r. Endicotts farm in ye place called Stikey Meadow which Land abovesaid I bought part of Deacon Tho Perkins about thirty acres & about thirty more which I bought of Daniell Borman, but in case y^t neither of ye children Kezia or Mercy shall live to ye age of eighteen y^t then ye abovesaid thirty acres apiece shall return to my next & immediate children to be equally divided amongst them & in case one of ye said grandchildren live to y^t age & not ye other that there ye whole threescore acres shall fall to ye surviver of them.

Item. I do give to my Son Nathaniell Pebody together with my Grandchild Samson How all that four hundred acres which I bought of M^r. Stephen Sewall Lying in Rowly village now called Boxford which land lyeth near Bradford & was formerly Mr. Nelsons of Rowly, my will is y^t my Son Nathaniell shall have three hundred & Samson How ye other hundred acres which for quantity & quality ye aforesaid Samson How shall have ye said Hundred acres provided y^t ye said Samson How shall be at my disposal till ye age of twenty one years But in case my Son Nathaniell shall dye without Lawfull Issue that then the abovesaid three hundred acres shall fall to my other children by equall division, his widdow notwithstanding injoying the benefit thereof during life & as to his movable estate which he is already in possession of I leave it all to be at his y^t is my son Nathaniells disposal here is to be understood y^t what shall be left undisposed of by my Son Nathaniell at his death of his three hundred acres shall be for y̆ᵉ use of his widdow, during her life as is abovesaid yᵗ is yᵉ life of her widdowhood.

Item. I do Reserve for Mary my wife ʸᵉ South End of my house for her use to live in as also ʸᵉ New Cellar as also yᵉ use of two milch Cowes which she shall choose out of my milch kine, Also my will is yᵗ my Son Isaac shall pay to my wife Mary, yearly twenty bushels of Indian Corn, four bushels of wheat, four of Rye & five of malt, also yᵗ my wife have liberty to keepe two or three swine, as also yearly half a dozen pound of wool, also my will is yᵗ my wife shall have pasture for her cowes with my son Isaacs as also yᵗ my Son Isaac shall provide fodder for them in ʸᵉ winter, As also yᵗ my wife shall have Liberty for an horse to ride on as she shall have occasion, Also my Will is yᵗ in case my Wife shall marry again yᵗ then all ʸᵉ priviledges abovesaid shall cease, but during her widdowhood she shall also have (as benefit by my orchard) yearly a barrell of Cider as also som apples as occasion either in the Summer or winter shall require, Moreover my wife shall have yᵉ use & disposal of two beds together with needful firewood provided her for which end she shall have ʸᵉ use of such of my oxen as shall be needfull, Also I do order yᵗ Samson How shall live with my Wife till he shall come to ʸᵉ age of twenty one years & be at her Command to be helpfull to her on all accounts as she shall have occasion & in case Samson How shall be taken away by his father before he shall have served as abovesaid yᵗ then my Wife shall have that hundred acres of land abovesaid (given conditionaly to ʸᵉ said Samson) to provide for herself such help as shall be necessary. & in case my Wife shall dye before ʸᵉ said Samson How shall arrive at yᵉ aforesaid term of years yᵗ then he shall be at my wives disposal to whom she shall see good and in case yᵉ said Samson will not comply with such dispose yᵗ then ʸᵉ said hundred acres of land intended for him shall be at my wives dispose.

Item. I give to my Daughter Lydia Perley five pounds besides what she hath already had of me.

I do give to my Daughter Mary Death five pounds besides what she hath had already I do give to my Daughter Sarah How five pounds besides what she hath had already.

Item. I do give to my Daughter Hephzibah Ray five pounds besides what she hath had already all which Legasies ordered to my children I do appoint to be paid in common currant pay as is before specified to other of my children.

Note y^t what Legasies I do here give in my will shall be paid by my executors out of my estate which I do leave in my Son Issacs hands & my wives, as corn or Cattell &c my debts & funerall expences being discharged.

And finally I do appoint, constitute & ordain my Wife Mary to be an executrix together with my Son John Pebody & Isaac Pebody as Executors of this my last will & testament & in Case after Legasies paid there be any estate left to be devided y^t it shall be disposed of in a way of division as my executrix together wth executors shall see good.

That what is here above written is ye last will & testament of ye abovesaid Francis Pebody appears by his own hand & Seal ye day & Date here mentioned as also by ye testimony of ye witnesses hereunto subscribed.

It is to be noted y^t notwithstanding what is abovesaid concerning my Son Nathaniels three hundred acres returning to his bretheren in case of his dying wthout lawfull issue, It is to be understood by the three hundred acres what he shall not see cause to dispose of before his death I hereby notwithstanding what hath been said giving him full power in case he see good to dispose of it either in part or whole not knowing but divine providence may necessitate him thereunto otherwise what is above written to be of full force as is expressed.

Francis Pebody.

The abovesaid Premises were signed & sealed & declared to be ye last will & testament of ye said Francis Pebody ye twentieth day of January in ye year of our Lord one thousand six hundred ninety & five or six in presence of us.

Joseph Capen,
Thomas Baker,
Ephraim Dorman, Senr.

FRANCIS PEABODY'S WILL.

Essex, ss. Before ye Honble Jonathan Corwin Esqr Judge of Probate of Wills &c at Salem Augst 7th 1698 Mr. Joseph Capen Mr. Thomas Baker & Mr Ephraim Dorman Senr p^rsonally Appeared and Made Oath that they were p^rsent & Saw Francis Pebody Sign and Seal and heard him Declare ye wth in Written Instram^t to be his Last will and testam^t & that he was then of a Disposing mind to the best of those Deserving and that they then Sett to there hands as Witnesses in ye p^rsence of ye Said Francis Peobody at Y^e Same time.

Sworne Attest John Higginson Reg^r.

Upon wch this Will is proved Approved and allowed being p^rsented by Mary Peobody Executrix & John Peobody & Isaac Peobody Executors therein named who Likewise Accepted of there Executorship.

Attest John Higginson Reg^r.

The Inventory of Y^e estate ffrancis pebody made this 20th of May, 1698.

two oxen at 7^l three Cowes at 9^l–15^s three young calves at 6^l	23–00–00
Sheep 4^l one mare and colt 1^l–10^s	05–10–00
chaines, axes, waggon, and chissels and other Iron tools	02–04–00
Wearing cloaths	02–04–00
3 beds and beding 12^l napkins tablecloths and other linnen at 5^l–9^s	17–09–00
chests, tables, chairs, and other lumber	05–15–00
pewter, and brass ware	05–12–06
Iron ware, as pots, kettles, tramells &c	02–05–00
new cloth home made	02–11–00
ten bus. of malt 1^l–15^s Indian Corne eight bus. 1^l–4^s Six bushels barley 1^l–1^s	04–00–00
four swine	02–00–00
Land given to his son John pebody,	200–00–00
Land given to Joseph pebody,	100–00–00
Land given to Nathaniell pebody,	150–00–00

Land given to Samson How,	050–00–00
Land given to Keziah and Mercie pebody,	050–00–00
Land and house to Jacob pebody,	160–00–00
the homestead to Isaac pebody upland and meadow dwelling house and one barne and mill,	400–00–00
Silver money,	044–15–00
totall summ	1327–05–06

William Howlett,
Daniel Redington,
Ephraim Wildes.

Topsfield ye 30th of September 1698.

In addition to the inventory of the estate of ffrancis pebody as doth apear on the other side of this paper:—

two oxen att	09–00–00
nine books	00–13–00
two cowes	06–00–00
two oxen	08–00–00
two linen Spinning wheels	00–06–00
two wolen Spinning wheels	00–06–00
two beds with the Furniture given to ye widow	19–00–00
Eaight yards woll cloath	01–12–00
Six Cushions	00–06–00
bed and beding given to Isaac	03–10–00

Daniel Redington,
Ephraim Wildes,
Joseph Bysbe.

NEWSPAPER ITEMS RELATING TO TOPSFIELD.

COPIED FROM THE FILES OF SALEM NEWSPAPERS

BY GEORGE FRANCIS DOW.

(Continued from Vol. V (1899), page 142.)

Post Office, Salem, Mass. Winter arrangement of the Mails. Haverhill & Topsfield,—arrive every Thursday at 10 o'clock, A. M. Depart same day at 2 o'clock, P. M. Letters must be left one quarter of an hour previous to the period of departure.

Salem Register, Jan. 7, 1805.

Post Office, Salem, Mass.

Winter arrangement of mails.

HAVERHILL & TOPSFIELD MAILS.

Arrive every Thursday at 10 o'clock A. M. Depart same day, at 2 P. M. Letters must be left one quarter of an hour previous to the period of departure herein mentioned.

Salem Gazette, Jan. 11, 1805.

David Towne advertised that he had been appointed administrator of the estate of Archelaus Towne, housewright, and Eunice Towne, a single-woman, both of Topsfield.

Salem Gazette, Feb. 8, 1805.

PURSE LOST.

Lost, a blue PURSE, containing some change, and a Note of Hand for *seventy dollars*, signed by Nathaniel Wells, and witnessed by Daniel Towne, jun. Whoever will return the same to the subscriber, shall receive a handsome reward.

Daniel Perkins.

Topsfield, Feb. 5.

Salem Gazette, Feb. 8, 1805.

In the late Grand Democratic Legislative Caucus at Boston, it was urged as an essential point, that the most cunning measures should be taken completely to revolutionize the *County of Essex*. To effect this, it was agreed that it would be expedient to begin with the March meetings, so that suitable persons might be chosen into the town offices to facilitate their victory in the April election; and that, for making the more minute arrangements, County and Town Caucusses should be previously held for that purpose. Pursuant to this plan, Democratic Deputies from various towns met yesterday at the Turnpike Hotel in Topsfield; where no doubt they agreed who should be our officers, and how they should rule us. In those towns where the Federalists are a majority, it will depend upon them whether the Demos shall carry all before them or not. Surely such measures to control and bind them ought to alarm them to a sense of their danger, and rouse them to action.

Salem Gazette, Mar. 1, 1805.

Dudley Wildes and Jabez Towne 3rd, commissioners, to receive claims against the estate of Jacob Ross late of Ipswich, yeoman, advertised to meet at the house of Nehemiah Cleaveland, Esq. innholder, Topsfield.

Salem Gazette, Apr. 26, 1805.

Topsfield, not choosing to obey the high-handed orders of the Boston Junto, have voted *not* to send a Representative to the General Court this year.

Salem Register, May 13, 1805.

DIED.—At Topsfield, on Wednesday last, Mr. Francis Skerry, aged 50; killed by the falling of a large quantity of earth from the bank at Topsfield hill, while at work upon the turnpike road, another man was much hurt at the same time so as to be obliged to have a leg amputated. One man was killed and two wounded, at the same place, and in the same manner, last summer.

Salem Gazette, July 26, 1805.

DIED.—At Topsfield, Mrs. Esther Estey, aged 100, relict of the late Mr. Aaron Estey. Early in her youth she became devoted to religion, and was a distinguished member of Christ's Church, for about eighty years. During which time she maintained a character comporting with her profession. As a wife she was kind, prudent and virtuous; she was an affectionate and instructive parent, a humane and indulgent mistress, a generous and obliging neighbor, and a faithful hospitable friend, at whose habitation wine and oil were poured into the wounds of the afflicted, and the indigent were not sent empty away. As a christian she was humble and submissive, yet zealous and active, placing all confidence in the merits of Jesus. She stood with loins girt about, and her lamp trimmed and burning, waiting with patience for that glorious day, when her Lord should call her from this vain world to shout forth ceaseless praises to her redeemer, in his kingdom of unfading felicity.

Salem Gazette, Aug. 20, 1805.

An alarm has gone forth that the *Yellow Fever* is in Lynn. We believe it is unfounded. Lynn is not more sickly than Wenham, Beverly, Topsfield, and other towns in this vicinity, have been this season. The mortality in these places has been great; but the disorder has not acquired the character of the Yellow Fever, and has abated.

Salem Gazette, Oct. 25, 1805.

DIED.—At Topsfield, Mrs. GALLOP, wife of Mr. Amos Gallop, aged 48; DANIEL GALLOP, son of Amos Gallop, aged 15; HIRAM CUMMINGS, son of David Cummings, aged 15; and (of Boxford) Mr. DANIEL BROWN, aged 27. These were all in one neighborhood; Mrs. Gallop and son were buried in one grave.

Salem Gazette, Oct. 25, 1805.

Robert Perkins of Topsfield gave notice of his appointment as administrator of the estate of Samuel Silver of Salem, mariner.

Salem Gazette, Dec. 3, 1805.

County Caucus.—We learn that the grand Essex Democratic Caucus, for the management of our elections, is to be holden at the Turnpike Hotel, in Topsfield—we have not heard when.

Salem Gazette, Jan. 28, 1806.

To the Democratic Republicans of Essex.

We are informed by the *Salem Gazette* that a COUNTY CAUCUS is to be holden at Topsfield, within a short time, to make arrangements for the Town, County and State Elections of the ensuing Spring.

With indignation many of you have doubtless witnessed for years past conventions of this nature; and your indignation is just, because an *undue influence* is used when two or three men from each town in our County in secret are to form electioneering projects.

Are we not free agents? Did not our fathers shed their most precious blood, that we their posterity might enjoy, among other privileges, the right of *Free Election*?

Do the enlightened people of Essex wish to be informed yearly, by a vain, self created society, on whom to bestow their suffrages for Governor, Senators, Town Officers, &c.— Are we not able to purchase newspapers and thereby gain information of the conduct of our public men—better information than we can obtain from the resolves of a secret caucus meeting?

What else can be the object of these meetings than to destroy the *Freedom of Election*, by exciting us to act, being ourselves ignorant of the true motives of our conduct?

My friends, let us examine with a cautious eye the conduct of our public servants—Let us reward them with our confidence in proportion to their merits—and to obtain the knowledge of their merits, let us read the various public papers, and use the other public means which are in every man's power.

When a man is boldly acting on the stage of public life, let us candidly and honorably adjudicate him, instead of basely seeking information from his invidious and secret enemies.

The object of this short address is to induce all, in their great political concerns, to make the best improvement of the reason and judgement which God has given them, and to caution every one who may be invited to attend the ensuing secret meeting, to *refuse* with an independent and manly spirit. The design of this meeting cannot be virtuous, otherwise it would not shun the eye of public observation. If it were honorable you would receive a *public* notification to attend. If it be your serious wish to promote the cause of *Democracy*, you can do this without attending a caucus. If you attend, you will go to it without self approbation, be ashamed of your company while there, and return home in conscious disgrace.

Let every gentleman in the County, who may be invited to attend, consider whether it will not most promote his honor and happiness to remain at HOME, enjoying the company of his wife and children, and an unsuspicious intercourse with *all* his friends and neighbors.

A FRIEND.

Salem Gazette, Feb. 4, 1806.

The federal town of Topsfield have voted as usual, not to send a Representative this year.

Salem Gazette, May 9, 1806.

WHEREAS the subscriber gave his Note of Hand, bearing date the 17th March, 1806, for sixty-two dollars and about 70 cents, to *Andrew Elliot*, of *Middleton*, and said note has since been paid but not taken up—this is to caution all persons against buying the same, as it will not be again paid if presented.

Topsfield, May 9. JOHN BALCH.

Salem Gazette, May 9, 1806.

In Topsfield, Nathaniel Hammond, Esq., a federalist, has been chosen to represent that town in the next General Court.

Salem Register, May 19, 1806.

DIED.—At Topsfield, Master ELIJAH PERKINS, son of Mr. Zebulun Perkins, aged 15.

Salem Gazette, May 27, 1806.

Notice is hereby given that the subscribers have been appointed by the Hon. Samuel Holten, Esq., Judge of Probate, Guardian of DANIEL PERKINS, JUN., of Topsfield, a person given to excessive drinking, &c. All persons are hereby forbid trading with or trusting him, as we shall not pay any debts of his contracting.

Daniel Bixby,
Ezra Perkins.

Topsfield, Sept. 14, 1806.

Salem Gazette, Sept. 19, 1806.

RAN AWAY.

From the subscriber, a Prisoner by the name of HENRY WOODS, about 25 years of age, about five feet and nine inches high, and light complexion, short hair. Whoever will take up said prisoner, and deliver him to the said subscriber, shall receive TEN DOLLARS reward.

SIMON GOULD.
Constable of Topsfield.

Topsfield, Sept. 23.

Salem Gazette, Sept. 23, 1809.

MARRIED.—At Topsfield, by the Rev. Mr. Huntington, Mr. Ephraim Wildes, jun., to the amiable Miss Rachel Towne.

Salem Gazette, Apr. 17, 1807.

DIED.—At Topsfield, suddenly, Mr. JACOB TOWNE, 80.

Salem Gazette, Sept. 29, 1807.

Of the several bills of mortality produced in this neighborhood, the result seems most favourable to Topsfield, as the number of early deaths is least, and the proportion to the population most favorable.

Salem Register, Jan. 26, 1807.

LOST, on Friday, the 27th March, between Salem and Topsfield, a SADDLE, with a sheep-skin on the under part. Any person who has found it and will give information so that it may be obtained, shall be handsomely rewarded by
                               Joseph Cree.
Salem Register April 6, 1807.

Summer course of the mails, from Salem, Mass. Topsfield and Haverhill mails arrive every Saturday, at 11 o'clock, A. M.—Depart at 2 o'clock, P. M., on the same day.
                       Salem Register, June 15, 1807.

To the Senate and House of Representatives of the Commonwealth of Mass.—Humbly show the Selectmen of the town of Topsfield, that the inhabitants of said town for a number of years last past have been at trouble and expence with other towns through which Ipswich river runs to facilitate the passage of the fish that have their periodical return for running therein, and divers laws have been passed to favor the same, though your petitioners conceive there is still a deficiency in these laws whereby they may enjoy their just rights to which by nature and reason they are entitled.

That for many years last past an abundance of shad have been in said river at the usual time of running said fish, and your petitioners have not liberty to take any thereof by reason of a restraining charge in a law passed the 28th March 1788, which subjects the person or persons who make use of a seine or drag net to take any fish in said river or the streams running thereinto to the penalty of £20. That by reason of the width of said river and the depth of the water therein no fish can be taken unless by seine or drag net.—

Whereof your petitioners pray your honours to take the premises into your wise consideration and grant them the liberty of making use of a seine or drag net one day in a week in taking those fish and under such rules, regulations and restrictions as your honors shall deem right, and as in duty bound shall ever pray.

Josiah Lamson,
David Perkins,
Nathaniel Hammond,
Robert Perkins,
John Peabody.

Selectmen of Topsfield.

The above petition was printed by order of the Senate and House of Representatives.

Salem Gazette, Nov. 10, 1807.

WHEREAS my wife *Olive* has left my bed and board. This is to warn all persons not to trust her on my account, as I will not to pay any debts she may contract.

Topsfield, Dec. 14, 1807. ISRAEL CLARK.

Salem Gazette, Dec. 18, 1807.

Bill of Mortality for Topsfield for 1807.

Jan. 16, a son of T. Perkins, jr. aged 2 years—March 13, Mr. Daniel Dodge, 56—May 19, a son of E. Lake, jr, 2—Aug. 7, Mr. Moses Perkins, 75—Sept. 9, Mrs. Polly Lake, 45—14th, Mr. Jacob Averill, 79; Mrs. Hannah Balch, 81—18th, Mr. Jacob Towne, 80—Oct. 19, Mr. Thomas Moore, 77—Nov. 22, Mr. John Bradstreet, 90—Dec. 6, Mrs. Mary Hood, 80—11th, Mrs. Rachel Towne, 58—14th, Mrs. Elizabeth Towne, 86.

Salem Register, Feb. 6, 1808.

Summer course of the Mails to and from Salem, Ms. until Nov. 1, 1808.

Mail from Haverhill, Ms. and Topsfield every Saturday, at 11 o'clock; same day, returns at 2 o'clock, P. M.

Salem Register, May 4, 1808.

To the Honorable Justices of the Court of Sessions to be holden at Ipswich, within and for the County of Essex, on the second Tuesday of May, A. D., 1808, by adjournment from the second Tuesday of April in the same year.

Humbly shew the subscribers that last May they petitioned the Selectmen of the Town of Topsfield, in the said County, to lay out a private way for their own accommodation, beginning on the North side of the River, in said Topsfield, where a bridge is begun, through land of Messrs. Ezra and David Perkins, in the most convenient route to the Road, by the said Perkins' stating in their said petition that the same road which they prayed for, was convenient and necessary for them the said petitioners, and requested that it might be laid out of a suitable width. That on the fourteenth day of February last past, the said Selectmen of the said Town of Topsfield refused to lay out the said way, as by a record of their proceedings in this behalf will appear;—Whereupon your Petitioners humbly pray this Honorable Court to cause the said way to be laid out in due form of law, and the plan and course of the said private way to be ascertained and the damages, (if any) estimated as the law requires, to be paid by the Town of Topsfield, if it be deemed to be of general benefit; otherwise by the individual or individuals, for whose use and benefit the said way shall be laid out; and as in duty bound shall ever pray.

Joshua Town,
and one hundred and eighteen others.

[The Court ordered an appearance at the Ipswich Court holden on the second Tuesday in October, and also appointed Col. Israel Hutchinson of Danvers, Major Asa Nelson of Rowley, and Eleaser Putnam, Esq. of Danvers, a committee to view the premises.]

Salem Register, June 4, 1808.

Rev. Mr. Huntington of Topsfield delivered the prayer at the installation of Rev. Mr. Briggs over the first parish church in Boxford.

Salem Gazette, Sept. 30, 1808.

A Convention of Delegates from the several towns in the County of Essex was held at Topsfield yesterday—summoned by the present awful crisis of our country.

Salem Gazette, Oct. 7, 1808.

ESSEX RESOLUTIONS.

At a meeting of the DELEGATES from the several towns in the county of ESSEX, at Topsfield, on Thursday, October 6, 1808, assembled for the purpose of taking into consideration the alarming and ruinous condition of our public affairs, and of agreeing upon and recommending to the People such measures for obtaining constitutional relief and redress, as may be deemed expedient.

PRESENT.

FROM SALEM.

Jacob Ashton, Esq.
Hon. Benjamin Pickman, jr.
Capt. Joseph Peabody.
Capt. William Orne.
Philip Chase.
Samuel Ropes.

BEVERLY.

Hon. Israel Thorndike.
Thomas Davis, Esq.
Thomas Stevens, Esq.

NEWBURYPORT.

William Bartlett, Esq.
William Coombs, Esq.
Jonathan Gage, Esq.
Joseph Dana, Esq.
Daniel A. White, Esq.
Edward Little, Esq.
Thomas M. Clark, Esq.
Dr. Isaac Adams.
Daniel Burnham.

IPSWICH.

John Choate, Esq.
Nathaniel Lord, 3d.
Joseph Swasey, Esq.

NEWBURY.

Silas Little, Esq.

LYNN.

Frederick Breed, Esq.
Thomas Witt.
Samuel Brimblecom.
James Gardner, Esq.

GLOUCESTER.

Benjamin K. Hough.
Capt. Thomas Parsons.
Lonson Nash, Esq.
James Hayes.

ROWLEY.

Dea. Thomas Merrill.
Parker Cleaveland, Esq.

SALISBURY.

Samuel March, Esq.

WENHAM.

Samuel Blanchard, Esq.
Jacob Dodge.

MANCHESTER.

William Tuck, Esq.
Capt. Abiel Burgess.

HAVERHILL.

Israel Bartlett, Esq.
James Duncan, jr., Esq.
Zebulon Ingersol, Esq.

BRADFORD.

Hon. Nathaniel Thurston.
Thomas Savary, Esq.

BOXFORD.

Thomas Perley, Esq.
John Robinson, Esq.

METHUEN.

Dea. William Swan.

MIDDLETON.

Benjamin Peabody, Esq.

Daniel Fuller.

ANDOVER.

Hon. John Phillips, jun.
Timothy Osgood.

MARBLEHEAD.

Thomas Meek.
Nathaniel Hooper.
William Reed.
John Tedder.
Capt. Ward Blackler.
Henry Gallison.

TOPSFIELD.

Nehemiah Cleaveland, Esq.
Nathaniel Hammond, Esq.
Sylvanus Wilds, Esq.
David Perkins.

DANVERS.

Gideon Foster, Esq.
Jonathan Ingersol, Esq.
Capt. Thomas Putnam.

HAMILTON.

Rev. Dr. Manasseh Cutler.
Robert Dodge, Esq.

WILLIAM BARTLETT, *Esq.*, was chosen *Moderator*.
LONSON NASH, *Esq., Secretary.*

RESOLUTIONS, &c.

The following RESOLUTIONS *and* ADDRESS, *prepared and reported by a Committee appointed for that purpose, were unanimously adopted.*

Resolved, That although the right of the people peaceably to assemble and deliberate upon their publick affairs is not only unquestionable, and essential to the existence of a free government, but is expressly sanctioned and secured by the constitution; yet the members of this assembly, entertaining the highest respect for the laws, and unwilling, in ordinary times, to interfere with the measures of their constituted authorities, are of opinion that this solemn right ought never to be exercised but in moments of extreme publick danger, or of general and deep distress.

Resolved, That, in our estimation, such a moment is the present, with which nothing in the annals of our nation since the peace of 1783, can exhibit a parallel. From a state of prosperity of which there is no example; and which by a wise and prudent policy, we conceive, might have been continued, the nation, in a time of profound peace, is suddenly involved in the deepest calamity and distress.—Our exterior commerce, to which the people of the United States have an unalienable right, is, without any reasonable pretext, wholly interdicted; and this by a statute, in its legal operation, perpetual, and dependent for its repeal, not on the will of the majority of the nation, but on the discretion of a small number of individuals.

By this unprecedented act, adopted without notice, and apparently without justifiable motive, great numbers of individuals, in New-England, find themselves reduced from opulence to poverty; and the wide spreading mischief is felt with a greater or less degree of pressure under every roof in all the commercial States:—And, as if the total suspension of our foreign commerce, and the interdiction of our most important means of procuring subsistence, for an indefinite period, were not of itself an intolerable evil, the *manner* in which these measures have been enforced, a manner totally unnecessary for the avowed object of them, has been, if possible, more oppressive than the measures themselves.

To the patience, the coolness, and the regular steady habits of the people of New-England, a character, which, it is to be hoped, they will never forfeit, is to be attributed their quiet submission to measures, which, while Colonies, under the administration of a British minister, they would have repelled at every hazard.

To prevent a recurrence to measures, which nothing but an extremity of suffering, and the failure of all constitutional remedy could justify, this assembly has been convened.

It is equally our object to discountenance and discourage those impetuous and irregular efforts, to which despondency and despair might impel; as it is by firm, united, determined, and persevering exertions to obtain peaceable redress.

Since the President of the United States has not deemed it expedient, in compliance with the numerous petitions from the people of New England, to exercise the discretionary power vested in him for our relief; since, indeed, he has declared that he sees no occasion to change the present destructive policy;—it surely behoves the people, by vigorous and united appeals, to seek redress from the Legislature of the United States. If, notwithstanding these earnest suplications, the Congress should unhappily be found deaf or indifferent to the interests of the commercial states, and determined to sacrifice our dearest rights for visionary projects; we firmly rely for relief on the wisdom and patriotism of our state government, whom the people have placed as sentinels to guard our rights and privileges, from whatever quarter they may be invaded. We trust that *they* will take care that the Constitution of the United States be maintained in its *spirit*, as well as in its letter; and that if, by any latitude of construction, it can be deemed to have authorised any body of men to deprive us of our birthright, and of our dearest privileges, it may be so amended as to secure the nation from such evils in future.

Resolved, That such has been our suffering, and so great is our alarm occasioned by the extraordinary measures lately adopted, that we shall never be contented until we are secured from a repetition of the same evils. That a bare repeal of the obnoxious acts ought not, therefore, to satisfy a free and a prudent people, any more than the repeal of the British stamp act silenced the patriots of that day. That there ought to be a solemn renunciation of the rights thus assumed; and it is the opinion of this assembly that legal and constitutional measures should be adopted for that purpose.

Resolved, That when the rapid, secret and unprecedented manner in which the system of embargo laws was passed, is considered; when, in contempt of the reasons urged in the message which recommended it, the interdiction was extended to exportation by land, in which neither our resources nor our seamen were endangered; when it is considered that this latter prohibition principally operates on one of belligerents only; when we call to mind the spirited and manly declarations of many members of Congress, on the floor of that honorable body, some of whom have been always ranged under the banners of the administration, that these measures were adopted, if not in obedience, at least in complaisance to FRANCE; and when it is stated from high authority, that they fully meet the approbation of the French Emperor:—when the passage of the non-importation act and the hasty rejection of the treaty negotiated by Messrs. Munroe & Pinckney are recollected; in short, when reviewing the whole conduct of the present administration, it is perceived that their measures have uniformly evinced a partiality for, and subserviency to one nation and a deep rooted prejudice against another, highly unbecoming the character of rulers of a nation professing to be neutral, and still more highly injurious to our interests:—when too, we see all the zealous supporters of this administration endeavouring to rouse the People to a war with Great-Britain:—It is impossible for this assembly not to feel; (and feeling, they would disdain to suppress their sentiments,) that it is much to be feared, as well as deprecated, that the administration, though induced by the bold language of the people, and their prevailing dissatisfaction with the embargo, to repeal these obnoxious acts, will do it, in order if possible, to inflict a still more fatal wound in the bosom of our country; that either they will enter into an open war with Great-Britain or will pass such acts and adopt such measures, as will inevitably produce such a result.

This assembly declare it as their deliberate opinion that there exists no cause of war with Great-Britain; that such a war would be unjust, unnecessary, and extremely to be deplored; that the removal of the embargo will not necessarily involve us in war, but should this be the alternative, it ought to be a war with France and not with Great-Britain.

Inhabiting a part of the Union the most engaged in foreign commerce, they think themselves qualified to decide upon its risks, and the nature and extent of the injuries to which it is exposed; and it is their firm belief that our commerce, unrestrained by self-destroying measures, might find many sources of profitable employment, without interfering in any degree with those principals of maritime law, which Great-Britain deems essential to her existence, and which, in an eventful moment like the present, she will never yield.

And this assembly cannot refrain from expressing their conviction, that neither the honor nor the permanent interests of the United States require that we should drive Great-Britain, if it were in our power, to the surrendry of those claims so essential to her in the mighty conflict in which she is at present engaged; a conflict interesting to humanity, to morals, to religion, and the last struggle of liberty: For they conceive that should the brave and much injured Spaniards fail in the contest in which they are so nobly assisted by Great-Britain, there would exist no barrier to the ambition of France. The continent of Europe is making one convulsive effort whether it be, as we would most ardently hope, the crisis of the disease preceding convalescence, or the struggle of death, time only can determine.

Should Spain and Great-Britain fall, the world will own but a single master. The myrmidons of the conqueror, transported to New Spain, would soon be found unquiet neighbors of the United States. Our resistance, it is too much to be feared would be feeble and short lived; indeed, we are already half conquered by our divisions, and, incredible as it may seem, there are those among us who are infatuated with the delusion that the dominion of France is a providential blessing.

We therefore consider, that the policy of yielding, in *appearance* only, to the wishes of the people by taking off the Embargo, and at the same time exciting a war with Great Britain, cannot be to zealously deprecated.

That there is a course of dignity, of good faith and impartiality towards the belligerent power which will procure for us respect and safety; and that Peace may be preserved with all nations without the expensive and voluntary sacrifice of either our rights, our interests, or our honour.

Resolved, That while we are constrained to bear testimony against the policy of our national administration, as involving the sacrifice of our dearest rights, and tending to a dissolution of the national compact, we declare our cordial attachment to the Constitution of the United States, and our determination to support the UNION, at all hazards.

WILLIAM BARTLETT, *Moderator.*

TO THE PEOPLE OF THE COUNTY OF ESSEX.

FELLOW-CITIZENS,

WE have attended to the duty of our appointment, under a solemn sense of its importance, and we now present to you the result of our deliberations. Convinced as we are, that evils in their nature most serious, and in their extent incalculable, menace our common country, we feel constrained to sound the alarm. We earnestly invite and implore you to co-operate with us in such regular and constitutional methods as may tend to avert the dangers which hang over us.

We unequivocally declare our opinion that the Embargo must be raised, or the ruin of our country is inevitable.

That its removal will lay us under the necessity of going to war with either of the belligerent nations of Europe, we can not for a moment admit.

That the present administration are inclined to make war upon France will not be suspected. Nor is it possible for any intellegent and candid man in the community to believe we have any sufficient reason for war with England.

None of those points of controvercy, which have been so assiduously used as instruments of irritation, can at all justify the measure.

These may be comprised under the four following heads.
1. The restrictions of the colonial trade by Great-Britain.
2. The impressment of her seamen from our merchant vessels.
3. The attack on the Chesapeak. 4. The Orders of Council.

As to the colonial trade, what ever may be the precise limits of the rightful claims of the respective nations, Great-Britain has offered to stipulate such an arrangement, as would, during the present war, secure to the United States all the pecuniary advantages of this commerce, and leave the question of abstract right on both sides, unenlarged and unimpaired, for future discussion. An offer which seems to defy a refusal. (a)

As to the impressment of seamen, she claims only what every nation in Europe equally claims, and all of them, as well as the United States themselves, uniformly practise. She pretends to no right to molest the real seamen of the United States; and on this critical point, involving the defence of her very existence, she has offered what our ministers, men high in the confidence of the administration, thought reasonable and satisfactory. (b)

In regard to the affair of the Chesapeak, it is true that Americans should ever be ready to repel, at the hazard of life, an attack on a national ship; but, waving the provocation on our part, the British government has, in every form disavowed, and the British nation disapproved the act. An honorable embassy has been sent to heal a wound unintentionally given, and to make liberal reparation. This we have refused, while, contrary to right reason, and established usage, we have persisted in a feeble but offensive attempt of reparation of own choice.

As to the Orders of Council. It will be recollected that these orders, bearing date 11th Nov. 1807, were occasioned by the Decree of the French Emperor, dated Nov. 1806, declaring all the British dominions in a state of blockade. Great Britain may think these orders completely justified by the Lex Talionis (law of retaliation.) There is no reason to consider them as originating from a disposition hostile to this country, and they ought not to be so considered: It is notorious that she could, according to known laws and usage, plead the actual blockade, by her navy, of all the principal ports under the power of France.

Such being the state of things, it is our solemn and decided opinion, that should our national administration endeavor to plunge our country into a war with Great Britain, it would be the duty of every citizen to lift up his voice against it as equally unjust, impolitic and ruinous.

WILLIAM BARTLET, *Moderator*.

Attest

LONSON NASH, *Secretary*.

NOTES.

(a) On the subject of Colonial trade it is unquestionably true that Great Britain has offered what, even in the opinion of Mr. Jefferson, might be accepted consistently with the honor of the United States; although she prohibits the direct trade of neutrals between the mother country and the colonies of her enemies; the terms on which she offers to us the colonial trade through our own country, to the mother country of the colony, are as favorable as could be expected.

"We were authorized," says Mr. Munroe, "to stipulate if better conditions could not be obtained, that the goods should be landed, the duties paid, and the ship changed. "We stipulated only that the goods should be landed, and the duty paid, making the duty on European goods one per cent. and on Colony products two. By exempting the party from the necessity of changing the ship, an important advantage was secured."

See 11th art. of the rejected British Treaty—also, Monroe's Letter to James Madison, of Feb. 28, 1808, published in the Repertory of April 26 and 29, 1808, and in many other newspapers.

(b) "The idea entertained by the public, is, that the rights of the United States were abandoned by the American commissioners in the late negotiation, and that their seamen were left by tacit acquiescence, if not by formal renunciation, to depend for their safety, on the mercy of the British cruizers. I have, on the contrary always believed, and still do believe that the ground on which that interest was placed by the paper of the British commissioners of Nov. 8, 1806, and the explanations which accompanied it, was both honorable and advantageous to the United States. That it contained a concession in their favor, on the part of Great-Britain, on the great principle in contestation, never before made by a formal and obligatory act of the government, and which was highly favorable to their interests—and that it also imposed on her the obligation to conform her practice under it, till a more complete arrangement should be concluded, to the just claims of the United States." *Letter of Mr. Munroe, above cited.*

It were much to be wished that all the good people of the United States would make themselves thoroughly acquainted with the late British Treaty, rejected in so unprecedented a manner by the President, and with the important documents accompanying it, published by order of Congress.

Salem Gazette, Oct. 14, 1808.

Essex County.—We present to our readers this day, in the Resolutions and Address of the Federal Delegates convened at Topsfield the 6th inst., the sentiments of the body of this county upon our public affairs. The characters that composed that delegation, are such as have the deepest interest in the public welfare, and who can give no advice to their fellow citizens, which they do not religiously believe to be promotion of that object. The Resolutions they have passed, must be adopted by every sober citizen; and the opinion they have expressed in their address, that if the Embargo is not raised, the ruin of the country is inevitable, must be concurred in by every man not biassed by private interest, or some unaccountable prejudice.

Salem Gazette, Oct. 14, 1808.

Bill of Mortality for Topsfield, A. D., 1808.

June 21st, Lieut. Daniel Towne, aged 72 years.
July 13th, Mrs. Phebe Kimball, 60
Sept. 14th, Mrs. Ruth Bixby, 89
Oct. 28th, Mr. David Brown, 19
Nov. 4th, An Infant, 27 days.
" 5th, Miss Anna Gallop, 15

Salem Gazette, Jan. 17, 1809.

The Essex TORIES have advertised a Convention to be held on Monday next at Topsfield.

Salem Gazette, Feb. 17, 1809.

A Desperate Effort.—On Monday last there was a muster of the TORIES of the County of Essex at Topsfield, styling themselves a "republican convention." Great exertions had previously been made in all the towns in the County, to collect this meeting together; when assembled, behold what a collection of office-holders and hunters, and such men as they could influence to concur in their views! They passed a very long string of Resolves, which may be seen in the last Register. For bitterness and vulgarity we think they have never been equalled in this quarter. The leading purposes of them are, to encourage the Government to *continue the Embargo*, and to denounce the Whigs of Massachusetts as subjects of military execution, offering themselves, and five thousand able bodied men of the County of Essex [unparalled impudence!] to aid in the bloody work.—We think the sanguinary spirit of these resolves exceeds any thing which has disgraced even the present session of Congress—Nelson and others have called for the bleeding system; but here are the bravoes who say, We are ready to do the deed. But we view it as a paroxysm of an expiring faction, and as cause of courage and confidence to the true Whigs of the country, —To their Resolves they have annexed a list of State and County Candidates for office at the April elections—LINCOLN for Governor; and VARNUM, who in Congress has lent all his *feeble* powers in support of the Embargo System, for Lieut. Governor.

Salem Gazette, Feb. 24, 1809.

The Essex Tory Convention at Topsfield. Long communications relating to it may be found in the Mar. 3, Mar. 7, Mar. 21, Mar. 24, Mar. 28, Apr. 8, Apr. 14, Apr. 18, May 2, May 16, May 26, June 2, and June 16, issues of the Salem Gazette.

Abigail Floyd.

Informs her friends and the public, that she will open a SCHOOL on the first Monday in April, in the chamber over Mr. Stearn's store, Essex street, formerly occupied by Mr. Blydon for that purpose, where she will teach Reading, Writing, Arithmetic, English Grammar, Rhetoric, Composition and Needle Work—Also an intermediate School, from 11 to 1 o'clock. [Miss Floyd afterwards taught a private school in Topsfield.—G. F. D.]

Salem Gazette, Mar. 17, 1809.

TOPSFIELD HOTEL.

The subscriber respectfully informs the public, that he has taken the Hotel in Topsfield, hereby soliciting their patronage; promising travellers and parties of pleasure every attention and accomodation in his power, and particularly he invites the attention of invalid and other ladies and gentlemen, who may choose to spend any part of the Summer in the country, to the elevated, salubrious and delightful situation of the Hotel, and the large and pleasant chambers which he wishes to appropriate to their use.

Topsfield, May 2, 1809. EPHRAIM WILDES, jun.

Salem Gazette, May 2, 1809.

Mr. Cushing.

An able writer in your paper has gone through an examination of the late *"Tory Convention at Topsfield."* A publication of the *Names* of all the Delegates to that Convention seems to be now the only thing wanting to complete the exposition; and if you will call on your friends in the several parts of the county, no doubt a tolerably correct list might be formed, by the individuals collecting the names of the delegations to that *"multitudinous* assembly" from their respective towns. To annex the *characters* to names, would be unnecessary. *One* column might in this way be furnished, which I have no doubt would be of great utility. I therefore think the object well worth your attention.

SCRIBLERUS.

☞We like the hint of our correspondent, and would thank any of our friends, who have it in their power, to contribute to the object.—*Editor.*

Salem Gazette, June 20, 1809.

A "scribbler" in the Gazette wishes to know who the Delegates to the "Tory Convention at Topsfield" were, and the editor of that paper requests their names. Here they are:— [See Gazette under date of Oct. 14, 1808, for list of names here printed.] These are the names of the Delegates to the "Tory Convention at Topsfield;" and we think ourselves entitled to the "thanks" of the editor of the Gazette for furnishing them to his hand.

Salem Register, June 21, 1809.

Topsfield, May 18th, 1810.

Whereas Ally my Wife has behaved in an unbecoming manner and refused my bed and Board; this is to caution all persons not to harbour or trust her on my account, as I will not pay any debts of her contracting from the date hereof.

Sam'l Braisdell.

Salem Register, June 2, 1810.

A Bill of Mortality of Topsfield, 1809.

April 25th, Mrs. Lydia Fisk, aged 66 years.
May 12th, Miss Lydia Pike, aged 19 years.
Sept. 6th, An Infant.
27th, Nancy Lake, aged 6 years.
Dec. 3d, Mrs. Elizabeth Perkins, aged 100 years.

It affords matter of serious and gratefull reflection, that of a population of 800 persons, so few instances of death have taken place in this town the last year.

Salem Gazette, Jan. 19, 1810.

NOTICE is hereby given, that the subscriber has been duly appointed Guardian to DANIEL PERKINS, jun, of Topsfield, a person addicted to intemperance and idleness, and has taken upon himself that trust by entering into the requisite bonds. All persons are therefore forbid to trust said *Daniel Perkins, jun*, as I shall not pay any debt he may contract.

Topsfield, March 16, 1810.   JONAS MERRIAM.

Salem Gazette, March 20, 1810.

In the April 13, 1810 issue of the Salem Gazette, appears the notice of a legislative hearing on the petitions of the selectmen of Topsfield, Middleton, Reading and Wilmington, "that they have been at great expence to facilitate the passage of fish called Shad and Alewives in Ipswich river (so called), and that for several years past, those fish called Shad have in their season been plenty in said river; and as by the law of March 28th, 1788, the said inhabitants are prohibited the use of a seine or drag net to take said fish, and as there are not any narrows or falls in said river, within the limits of said towns, in which the said inhabitants can take fish with what is called a dip net, they are wholly deprived any advantage or profit whatever from said fish. Wherefore your petitioners pray the Honorable Court to grant by law to the inhabitants of said towns, the privilege of using a seine or drag net, for the purpose of taking said fish called Shad, one day in each week," etc.

DIED. At Topsfield, Mrs. Mary Cleaveland, relict of Rev. John Cleaveland, of Ipswich, aged 80. Remarkably endeared to her numerous acquaintances by the mildness of her temper—by her friendly attention to all, and by the very acceptable manner of her habitual acts of charity. She was a lover of the holy scriptures—a devout worshipper of God, and most happily supported the christian profession. Though of blameless conversation coupled with fear and singular meekness, yet she plead not her innocence as the ground of her hope. Her enlightened and humbled mind was so deeply impressed with just apprehensions of the purity of God, that she found no excellence in herself on which to rest. Her heart embraced the dispensations of grace, and her hope fixed on her prevalent Intercessor with the Father. She lived as seeing him who is invisible, and died in the exercise of the same faith and hope.

Salem Gazette, May 4, 1810.

A NEW STAGE will start next Monday from *Salem* for *Haverhill*, and return again the next day, and perform the same route three times a week. This will accommodate travellers to the northern parts of New-Hampshire, as at *Haverhill* it will meet the Stage from *Boston* for *Concord* and *Hanover*. Such carriages and horses will be employed as to render the travelling easy and expeditious. Passengers will apply at Perley's tavern in Salem, and Kendall's in Haverhill.

MORSE & FOX.

Salem Gazette, August 17, 1810.

SALEM AND HAVERHILL STAGE.

The Subscribers hereby give notice that they have commenced running a stage between Salem and Haverhill, in which undertaking they respectfully solicit the public patronage. The Stage starts from Salem on Mondays and Fridays, at 6 o'clock, A. M.—stops for breakfast at Topsfield Hotel, at half past 7, passes through Boxford and Bradford, and arrives in Haverhill at 10 o'clock, where it meets the Stage from Boston on its way through Concord and Hanover (N. H.) to Burlington, Vt.

It starts from Haverhill on Tuesdays and Saturdays, at 2 o'clock, P. M. (before which time the Boston Stage above mentioned arrives on its return) passing through the same places as in going, and arrives in Salem at 6 P. M. Slates for the reception of names are lodged at Messrs Tucker's and Perleys Taverns in Salem, and at Mr. Kendall's in Haverhill.

This is the shortest and most expeditious route to the FRANCONIA IRON WORKS, the road is good, and running through a fine country, will be an agreeable summer excursion for the purpose of health or pleasure. Good horses and careful drivers will be furnished, and every attention paid to passengers.

MORSE & FOX.

N. B. Trunks, Packages, etc., will be carefully attended to, and delivered, and all orders punctually executed.

Salem Gazette, Aug. 31, 1810.

DIED, In Topsfield, MR. ZEBULON PERKINS, aged 70. His situation for the last thirteen years has presented a rare instance of that extremity of suffering under which human life may be sustained. The first four years of his indisposition he experienced a general and increasing debility; this was attended with a contraction and distortion of his limbs, with great pain and helplessness, and an almost entire loss of speech. For the last nine years he has been unable to feed himself, or to move on his bed. For every attention in his position, he has been dependent on the aid of his friends,— "*Verily man in his best estate is altogether vanity.*"

Salem Gazette, Oct. 5, 1810.

The Bill of mortality from Topsfield [for the past year] has been uncommonly favorable to longevity giving a mean of above 70 years to all the deaths reported.

Salem Register, Jan. 30, 1811.

NOTICE. The subscriber has been duly appointed Guardian of AMMI AVERELL, of Topsfield, Yeoman, all persons are therefore forbid harboring or trusting the said Ammi on my account, as I will pay no debts he may contract.

Topsfield, Dec. 2, 1811.   Moses Averell, Guardian.

Salem Register, Dec. 3, 1811.

Daniel Bixby and Amos Perley having been appointed commissioners to receive and examine the claims of creditors of the estate of Jacob Andrews, late of Boxford, advertised their attendance at the dwelling-house of Nehemiah Cleaveland of Topsfield on the last Monday in each month.

Salem Gazette, April 5, 1811.

Notice is hereby given, that the Subscriber has been appointed Guardian to BENJAMIN KIMBALL, of Topsfield, blacksmith, a person who by excessive drinking and idleness does unreasonably spend and waste his Estate, and has accordingly taken upon himself that trust by giving bonds according to law. All persons therefore are hereby cautioned against trusting said Benjamin Kimball in future, as I shall not pay any debts he may contract after this date.

SAMUEL HOOD, *Guardian.*

Salem Gazette, April 19, 1811.

MARRIED. In this town, by the Rev. Dr. Hopkins, Mr. Joseph Emerson of Topsfield, to Miss Lydia Burrill, daughter of the late Mr. Ezra Burrill of this town.

Salem Gazette, April 26, 1811.

The citizens of Newburyport, in town meeting assembled, passed a vote of thanks to the people of various towns, Topsfield being named, who "flew to our assistance, as soon as information of our distress was given." i. e. the great fire whereby about 250 buildings were destroyed.

Salem Gazette, June 4, 1811.

The stage between Salem and Haverhill runs regularly under the direction of Richard Morse, the copartnership between Richard Morse and Ebenezer Fox having been dissolved.

Salem Gazette, June 25, 1811.

COURSE OF THE MAILS. To and from Salem, from Nov. 1, 1811, to May 1, 1812, . . . Haverhill & Topsfield Mail—Arrives every Saturday, at 10 o'clock, A. M.—Departs on the same day, at 1 o'clock, P. M. . . .

John Dabney, Post Master.

Salem Gazette, Dec. 10, 1811.

FOR SALE. A Farm, containing about one hundred acres, with a Dwelling House and other Buildings thereon, very pleasantly situated in the town of Topsfield, in the county of Essex, near the Turnpike Bridge, on the Road from Boston to Newburyport.
For further particulars inquire of

John D. Treadwell, at Salem.

or Charles Cleaveland, at Boston.

Salem Gazette, Jan. 24, 1812.

FEDERAL CONVENTION. We understand a convention of Federal Delegates from the several towns composing what is *called* Essex South District will be held at Topsfield Hotel on Monday next, to agree in a nomination of three Senatorial candidates. The towns composing this misshapen district are Salisbury, Amesbury, Haverhill and Methuen, at the *nothern* extremity; Andover, Middleton, Danvers, Lynnfield, Salem, Marblehead and Lynn, reaching to the *Southern* extremity, of the county; and Chelsea, in the County of Suffolk.

Salem Gazette, March 20, 1812.

A Court Martial will be held at Topsfield Hotel on the 24th inst. for the trial of Capt. Samuel Griffin, of the 5th Regiment, 2d. Division.

Salem Gazette, March 20, 1812.

In the April 28, 1812 issue of the Salem Gazette appears the advertizement of a legislative hearing to consider the petition of John Peabody, Jacob Towne, jr. and Jonas Merriam, selectmen, and Daniel Bixby, David Balch, Robert Perkins and Ephraim Wildes, jr. fish commitee, of Topsfield, and the selectmen, and in several instances the fish committee, of Boxford, Hamilton, Wenham, Danvers, Middleton, and Reading, asking for legislation to regulate the shad and alwife fishing in the Ipswich river and the streams running into the same. "That no person be allowed at any time to take any of said fish within twenty rods of any sluice way or mill dam in said river and said streams, that no person shall make any wall or place any other obstruction in said river or streams, which may in any way retard the passage of said fish or use any machinery for taking said fish which is not allowed by law, nor in any place except such as are appointed and authorized by the fish committee of the respective towns, that no person be allowed to take any of said fish in said river and streams running into the same, between sun-setting and sun-rising."

A NOTE OF HAND, given by Samuel Fowler, jun., of Danvers, in favor of the subscriber, the 14th June, 1811, for the sum of 193 dolls. 81 cents, with an endorsement upon it of 20 dolls. having been LOST (probably in Salem) sometime since the 11th of July last; this is to request any person who may have found the same, to return it to the subscriber, for which he shall be handsomely rewarded.

Topsfield, Aug. 18, 1812.   Josiah Gould.

Salem Gazette, Aug. 18, 1812.

DIED. In Topsfield, Miss Ruthy Ray, in the 38th year of her age, a native of that town, but for several years past resident in Marblehead. It would be injustice to the character of the deceased to suffer the remembrance of her worth to pass unnoticed into the oblivion of the grave. Amiable in her deportment, affable in her temper, discreet in her manners, pure in her morals, and sincere in her religious professions, she had the esteem of all who knew her, and, we trust, by her virtuous life, has gone to a better world, to reap the rewards of her redeemer's sufferings.

Salem Gazette, Nov. 3, 1812.

By order of the Circuit Court of Common Pleas begun and holden at Ipswich within and for the County of Essex, on the third Monday of December, A. D., 1812, will be sold at Public Auction on Wednesday the twenty-seventh day of January instant, one o'clock, P. M., the following parcels of Real Estate late of Joseph Andrews, of Topsfield, in said County, yeoman, deceased, intestate—to wit.

A piece of woodland in Boxford in said county, containing about ten acres, adjoining the road which leads from Jesse Perley's to Low's Saw Mill and bounded by land of Capt. Solomon Low, Dorothy Andrews, Jesse Perley and Hepzibah Andrews.

Also, about one acre of Peat meadow, in Topsfield in said County, at Hassocky meadow, so called, bounded by land of Robert Perkins, David Perkins and the heirs of Nathl. Averill and of Jacob Towne, junr.

Also, about two acres of salt marsh lying in Ipswich in said County, at a place called the Hundreds.

The sale will begin on the piece of Wood Land in Boxford; and the other parcels of the estate will be sold at the late dwelling house of the deceased in Topsfield.

Topsfield, Jan. 1, 1813.   Jacob Towne, Jun., Adm'r.

Salem Gazette, Jan. 1, 1813.

Died. Lost overboard from schr. Nancy, bound from Eastport to Portsmouth, a passenger by the name of Wright, said to belong to Topsfield, had been a prisoner and absent from home some time.

Salem Gazette, Jan. 12, 1813.

All persons having any demands on the estate of Major JOSEPH DORMAN, late of Topsfield, deceased, testate, are desired to exhibit the same, and all persons indebted thereto are requested to make payment immediately to the subscriber, or her attorney Sylvanus Wildes.

Topsfield, Jan. 22, 1813.   Phebe Dorman, Executrix.

Salem Gazette, Jan. 22, 1813.

In the Salem Gazette of Feb. 26, 1813, is printed a communication suggesting the nomination of Nathaniel Wade for the office of County Treasurer. The editor adds the following:—We have since received a similar recommendation of the Hon. NEHEMIAH CLEAVELAND, Esq. and three or four others have also been mentioned to us.

A FARM FOR SALE. To be Sold at Public Auction, at the house of the Subscriber, on Monday next, the 26th instant, at 9 o'clock, A. M. if not sold before at private sale, A valuable farm, situated in Topsfield, about a mile west of the meeting-house, containing 120 acres of Land—thirty acres of which are richly covered with excellent wood and timber, in a very thrifty state,—the residue consists of land for mowing, tillage, pasturage and orcharding, conveniently apportioned;—on which is a good Dwelling-House, a large Barn, a Shop, Granary, Chaise-House, Cyder-Mill and House, with other Out-Buildings, all lately erected, pleasantly situated, and in good repair.

Persons wishing to purchase said Farm are requested to view it prior to the day of sale.

SIMON GOULD.

Salem Gazette, April 20, 1813.

OBITUARY NOTICE OF THE REV. MR. HUNTINGTON.

Died.—In Topsfield, April 22, by a short and distressing illness, the Rev. Asahel Huntington, in his 53d year, greatly lamented.

On this mournful event, one of his brethren in the vicinity, writes thus: "If there was a minister in this circle, who might justly be called *amiable*, and "of an excellent spirit," such was that man, in all the relations of private life, and in the whole of his public character. My heart sinks when I think what a brother and friend I have lost; what the association, and the neighboring societies, have lost:—What then his consort, his children, and the bereaved flock!—He was a most pleasant and interesting companion. And if there was any where a *feeling* heart, alive to the claims of friendship, compassionate to all suffering and sorrow, such was *his* heart. If there was an Israelite indeed, of christian simplicity and sincerity, great integrity, and open-hearted benevolence, without a shadow of affectation—such was this excellent man. As a minister, he well understood, and well maintained the important realities of gospel revelation; delivered them in love, and carried them to their practical uses, with great fidelity, in a conciliating manner; and with much sensibility (according to the nature of every subject) though in "a still small voice," with no outward show or parade. And Topsfield will know—his hearers in every place will know, the more they consider him—"that there has been a prophet among them." Indeed, he had much of originality. But it was modest, unassuming, always submissive to scripture authority; and always aiming to desire its conception from that source. He had a fruitful mind; and in his discourses there was an uncommon variety of subjects and of sentiment. He was likewise distinguished by an acute discernment of men and things. By his instructive and interesting sermons, by his piety and purity of life, by a spirit of substantial kindness which went every where with him; by his humility, and great meekness of wisdom, he has been, more than 23 years, an important bond of union among a people, who *had been* disunited. It is hoped that their union will continue. The remembrance of *him* will do much to maintain it. A general undissembled grief appears now to prevail among them. And it is presumed they will long remember him. It is certain, that if they so cherish his memory as to imbibe his spirit, they will be a most happy society.

Salem Gazette, May 7, 1803.

SALEM LIGHT INFANTRY. On Tuesday afternoon last, this Military Company, . . . marched out of town, attended by their baggage-waggon, and as completely equipped with everything necessary to keep the field, as any corps in actual service. On Tuesday evening they encamped at Wenham; on Wednesday continued their march through Hamilton, Ipswich and Rowley to Newbury, where they pitched their tents that night, and on Thursday morning marched into Newburyport. . . . Towards evening they left Newburyport, and marched to their encampment in Newbury, where they passed the night. On Friday morning they commenced their homeward march, and pitched their tents at night on the heights in Topsfield. Saturday morning, they resumed their march towards Salem, and in the course of the forenoon were received with much hospitality and politeness at the house of our former townsman, Capt. Thomas Perkins of Topsfield. They arrived in town about three o'clock in the afternoon. . . .

Salem Gazette, June 15, 1813.

DIED. In this town, Mr. Gould, formerly of Topsfield.

Salem Gazette, June 25, 1813.

DIED. In Topsfield, Mr. Elijah Averell, aged 50; a worthy character.

Salem Gazette, Aug. 31, 1813.

Owners of carriages for the Conveyance of Persons who reside in Topsfield and other towns as named were notified to attend the office of Tristram Dalton, collector of revenue, "for the purpose of receiving Entries of such Carriages, and to Grant Certificates, on payment of the duties thereon required by law."

Salem Gazette, Jan. 1, 1814.

To be sold at Public Auction, by order of the Supreme Judicial Court, on Tuesday the 29th day of March next, at 1 o'clock, P. M., on the premises.

All the Real Estate of Alethea, Elisha, Asahel, Hezekiah and Mary Ann, minors and children of the Rev. Asahel Huntington, late of Topsfield, in said county, deceased, viz:

A Farm pleasantly situated in said Topsfield about half a mile from the meeting-house, containing about fifty-five acres of good Land, with a large well-finished Dwelling-House, Barn and other Buildings thereon, well watered and proportioned in tillage, mowing, orcharding and pasturage.

Also, a parcel of about three and a half acres of River Meadow and about one acre of Brook Meadow of excellent quality; two small lots of Peat Meadow, containing about one acre.

Also, one undivided fourth part of a small Farm, containing about 30 acres, with a Dwelling-House and Barn thereon, known by the name of the Tenney Place.

All the above parcels are situated in said Topsfield.

A lot of about two acres of Woodland in Boxford, and also one undivided half part of about 16 acres of Salt-Marsh in Ipswich, in a place called the Hundreds.

About 19 acres of the above named Lands, with part of the Dwelling-House and Out-Buildings, are set off and assigned to the widow of said deceased as her dower; the reversion of which will be included in the sale, and the widow will be willing to relinquish her dower for a reasonable consideration to be named at the time of sale.

At the same time and place will be sold, part of the Personal Estate, viz: 4 cows, one pair of steers, about 20 prime sheep, part of them half merino, and all likely to have lambs from a merino ram; Farming Implements, Household Furniture, &c.

N. Cleaveland, guardian to said minors, and adm'r of said Estate of said deceased.

Salem Gazette, March 1, 1814.

In the April 25, 1814 issue of the Salem Gazette appears the advertisement of a legislative hearing to consider a petition signed by the selectmen and fish committees of Topsfield and other towns bordering on the Ipswich river. The language of the petition is the same as that printed in the April 28, 1812 issue of the Gazette.

OXEN STOLEN. Stolen from a Pasture of the Subscriber, between the 16th and the 19th instant, a pair of six year old OXEN, with the yoke, one with a star in his forehead and rather spreading horns, the other rather dark horns; both of them red, and right ears cropt, left ears half cropt. Whoever will apprehend the thief, and return the cattle, shall be handsomely rewarded.

LYDIA WILDES.

Salem Gazette, June 21, 1814.

By order of Court, will be sold at Public Vendue, on 9th November next, at 2 o'clock, P. M. on the premises in Topsfield.

So much of the Real Estate of NATHANIEL CUMMINGS, late of Salem, in the County of Essex, blacksmith, deceased, as shall raise the sum of three hundred and twenty dollars, for the payment of his just debts and incidental charges. Said Estate consists of all that Pasturage, Meadow, and Woodland in Topsfield, devised to said Nathaniel by his father Capt. Thomas Cummings; and also a certain Wood-Lot in Wenham Swamp, consisting of about one acre and a half.— Terms and a particular description will be made known at the sale.

Salem, Oct. 18, 1814. MARY CUMMINGS, Adm'x.

Salem Gazette, Oct. 18, 1814.

LORD'S DAY. To unite the efforts of the friends of Morals and to devise a general system of measures, necessary to be pursued in executing the laws of the Commonwealth, with respect to the SABBATH; many friends of law and order in different parts of the County of ESSEX, have thought a CONVENTION advisable.

PUBLIC NOTICE therefore, is hereby given, that such a Convention will be holden at the Topsfield Hotel, on the third Wednesday of December inst. at 10 o'clock A. M. All the *Moral Societies* in the County are requested to send Delegates; and one or more *individuals* from every town in the County are respectfully invited to attend.

Salem Register, Dec. 9, 1814.

ESSEX CONVENTION. A Convention, composed of forty-three members, from thirteen different towns, was holden 21st Dec., 1814, at Topsfield Hotel, County of Essex, Mass., for the purpose of devising and adopting measures for the observation of the Lord's Day.

Hon. John Heard, Esq. was chosen Moderator; and Mr. John Adams, Clerk.

After the Convention was organized, the Throne of Grace was addressed on the occasion, by the Rev. Mr. Allen, of Bradford. Rev. Mr. Abbott of Beverly, Rev. Mr. Edwards of Andover, and Hon. Mr. Cleaveland of Topsfield, were chosen a Committee of Arrangements.

The Committee, after having attended to the duties of their appointment, reported for the consideration of the Convention the following Resolutions:

1. Resolved, That this Convention regard the Report of the Legislature of this Commonwealth in their session of June last, on the subject of the due observation of the Sabbath, with grateful respect; and devoutly wish there may be a concert of prudent and firm measures in all the towns of the County, to carry the recommendations of our civil fathers into full effect.

2. Resolved, That the early and discreet measures pursued by the public officers of several towns in this County, to restrain the violators of the Sabbath, meet with their warmest approbation and that they respectfully recommend to them to persevere in the same, till the important object be fully attained.

3. Resolved, That this Convention warmly recommend to the Tythingman and officers in other towns of the County, to engage in the prudent and faithful discharge of their duties with respect to the Lord's Day; and to give the more effect to their operations, to commence them on the first day of the New Year.

4. Resolved, That it be recommended to the friends of the Lord's Day in every town, to hold frequent meetings, for the purpose of extending support and countenance to public officers in the faithful discharge of their duties.

And as very much will depend on the wisdom, firmness and perseverance of the civil officers, whose duty it is to preserve the Sabbath from violation.

5. Resolved, That it be recommended to the friends of the Sabbath in every town, to make all honorable and prudent exertions to secure, in the coming Spring, the election of the best men to the office of Tythingmen: and to such men when elected, it is recommended, that no motives of personal convenience should induce them to shrink from the faithful discharge of their important duties.

6. Resolved, As the opinion of this convention, that a mild but faithful and persevering execution of the measures now recommended, will, with the divine blessing, soon prevent those flagrant violations of the Sabbath, which in late years, especially since the commencement of the present unhappy war, have given it the appearance of a day devoted to business and pleasure; will secure undisturbed peace to worshiping assemblies; will have an important influence in producing a stricter regard for this Divine institution among the rising generation and the unreflecting; and contribute, we devoutly hope, to the return to the divine favor to our guilty and suffering country.

The foregoing resolutions were unanimously adopted.

The Rev. Dr. Worcester, of Salem, Capt. John Pearson, of Newburyport, Rev. Mr. Allen, of Bradford, Hon. Mr. Cleaveland, of Topsfield, Dea. Rantoul, of Beverly, Rev. Mr. Edwards, of Andover, were chosen a standing committee.

Rev. Mr. Edwards was chosen a delegate to attend the next meeting of the Middlesex Convention to be holden in Concord on the last Wednesday in January, 1815.

Voted, that the papers containing the doings of this Convention be committed to the Clerk, and that he be requested to procure their publishment in the public papers of Boston, Salem, Newburyport, and Haverhill.

Voted, That this convention be adjourned, to meet again at this place, on the last Wednesday of April next, at 10 o'clock, A. M.

John Heard, Moderator.
John Adams, Clerk.

Salem Gazette, Dec. 26, 1814.

Will be sold at Public Vendue, on THURSDAY the 2d day of February next, at 1 o'clock, P. M., if not previously sold at private sale. All the Real Estate of ELIJAH AVERELL, late of Topsfield, deceased, consisting of the Homestead, containing about 62 acres with a good Dwelling-House, Barn and other Buildings thereon; well fenced with stone wall; suitably proportioned in tillage, mowing, pasturage and orcharding; a good supply of water, with a considerable quantity of excellent Wood, pleasantly situated within about a quarter of a mile of Topsfield meeting-house.—Also a Lot of about 3 acres of fine English Mowing; a lot of about 2 acres of thrifty Wood-Land on Averell's island; about 2 acres of prime Peat Meadow; about 2 acres of Swamp Wood Land; about 3 acres of good River Meadow.—The time of payment will be made convenient to the purchaser. The sale to be at the late dwelling-house of the deceased. The premises may be viewed at any time previous to the sale, by applying to either of the subscribers.

JOHN GOULD, 3d.

JOHN LAMSON.

Salem Gazette, Jan. 13, 1815.

A Pair of Saddle Bags were found on the road between Boxford and Topsfield on Monday last, which the Owner may have by proving property and paying charges. Apply to the subscriber, in Andover, North Parish.

ENOCH PARKE.

Salem Gazette, Feb. 3, 1815.

To be sold at Public Auction, if not previously sold at private sale, on MONDAY the 27th of March next, at 9 o'clock, on the premises, A FARM, pleasantly situated in Topsfield on the road leading from Wenham and Hamilton to Lamson's bridge, so called, containing 40 acres, consisting of Mowing, Tillage, Pasturing, and Orcharding; and one acre and half of Wood Land lying in Wenham Swamp; with a Dwelling-House, Barn and other Out-Houses.—Said Farm is capable of keeping six Cows, a Horse and half dozen sheep. Also at the same time will be sold, 1 Horse and Sleigh, 4 Cows— and other articles. Said property belongs to the heirs of JONAS CUMMINGS. Conditions made known at the time and place of sale. Any persons wishing to view the premises will meet the Subscribers on Monday the 27th of the present month on the premises.

JOHN CHOATE,

JOSEPH CHOATE.

Salem Gazette, Feb. 17, 1815.

LOST. On Tuesday afternoon, 28th Feb. a Red Moroco POCKET BOOK, containing five promissory Notes, made payable to the Subscriber (the whole amounting to somewhat over 200 dollars), together with a number of other papers. The Pocket Book was wrapped in a piece of brown paper, and lost either in Salem or on the road to Topsfield. Whoever may have found it, and will return it to the subscriber, shall be handsomely paid for his trouble.

AZARIAH AVERELL.

Salem Gazette, March 3, 1815.

THE SABBATH. The Convention held at Topsfield Hotel on the 21st December last for the purpose of devising and adopting measures for the due observance of the LORD'S DAY, stands adjourned to *Wednesday, 26th April* inst. at 10 o'clock in the forenoon, at the Hotel in Topsfield. At which time and place Delegates from every town in the county of Essex are respectfully invited to attend.

Salem Gazette, April 11, 1815.

OBSERVANCE OF THE SABBATH. ESSEX CONVENTION, Convened at Topsfield, April 26, 1815, according to adjournment. Members from fifteen different towns were present, and united with the Rev. Dr. Spring in addressing the Throne of Grace. The following Report and subsequent Resolutions were then submitted to the Convention. [Report occupies nearly three columns of space in Gazette]. The Convention adjourned to the first Wednesday in October next, to meet at the same place at 10 o'clock, P. M.

Salem Gazette, May 16, 1815.

ESSEX CONVENTION. The Essex Convention for promoting the due observation of the Lord's Day, met at Topsfield, October 4th, 1815, according to adjournment. The standing Committee exhibited the following Report [which occupies nearly a column of space in the Gazette].

The Convention then adjourned, to meet at such time and place, as the Standing Committee shall think proper.

Salem Gazette, Oct. 31, 1815.

VITAL STATISTICS OF TOPSFIELD, MASS.,

FOR THE YEAR 1903.

BIRTHS.

1903.

Jan. 29. Gertrude Myrl, dau. of Albert Herman and Josie (Tinkham) Davison.

Feb. 8. Cedric Phillips, son of Harry Walter and Bessie Rebecca (Phillips) Gilman.

Feb. 20. Gordon Brown, son of Manuel Frederick and Florence May (Brown) Castle.

Mar. 11. —— —— dau. of Benjamin Walter and Lucy Randlett (Pingree) Fuller.

Mar. 22. —— —— dau. of Gilbert Symonds and Genie (McMeekin) Mason.

April 5. Earnest Albert, son of Frank F. and Dora Annette (Cook) Lefavour.

April 10. —— —— dau. of Timothy Joseph and Katherine Theresa (Leary) Hickey.

May 3. Ella Josephine, dau. of Joseph and Mary Louise (Peabody) Fuller.

May 11. Lillian May, dau of Hiram Leslie and Mary Louise (Murphy) Clay.

May 25. Olive Jenette Irene, dau. of Charles Warren and Annie D. (Bell) Andrews.

May 27. Helen Mabelle, dau. of Herbert and Alice Belle (Johnson) Lewis.

Aug. 2. Victor Paul, son of Byron and Mary Rebecca (Leavitt) Sanborn.

Nov. 11. —— —— dau. of George William and Annie Belle (Pitman) Burnham.

Nov. 18. Gertrude Veronica, dau. of Theodore Francis and Angelina Josephine (Mullen) Paquette.

Nov. 18. Benjamin Walter, son of Arthur Freeman and Leonie (Cruchet) Perkins.

Dec. 6. —— —— dau. of George Roderick and Mary Ann (McQuarrie) Deering.

Dec. 25. —— —— dau. of Charles Hobart and Mary Elizabeth (Collins) Lake.

Dec. 26. Porter Harvey, son of Porter Bradstreet and Harriet Louisa (Fish) Peabody.

MARRIAGES.

1903.

Jan. 8. { Robert Edward Westcott (Lowell), son of Robert, M. D., and Hannah Little (Noyes) Westcott.
Elizabeth Anna Chemist (Topsfield), daughter of Charles and Elizabeth Anna (Reid) Chemist.

VITAL STATISTICS FOR 1903.

MARRIAGES (Continued.)

Mar. 4.
- Thomas James Luxton (Topsfield), son of George and Mary Jane (Baglole) Luxton.
- Florence Anna Pierce (Topsfield), daughter of Stephen M. and Eliza A. (Perkins) Pierce.

Mar. 31.
- Arthur Freeman Perkins (Topsfield), son of David Pratt and Addie J. (Phillips) Perkins.
- Leonie Cruchet (Topsfield), daughter of Henri and Leontine (Tremblay) Cruchet.

April 14.
- James Francis Creedon (Topsfield), son of James B. and Anna (Powers) Creedon.
- Mary Agnes Sheehan (Boston), daughter of Jeremiah and Helen (Doherty) Sheehan.

May 7.
- Albert Merrill Dodge (Topsfield), son of John H. and Mary J. (Perkins) Dodge.
- Florence Melissa Dodge (Topsfield), daughter of C. Frederick and Huldah M. (Littlefield) Dodge.

June 23.
- Wendell Stewart Pace (Topsfield), son of Albert William and Ellen M. (Perkins) Pace.
- Angie Foster Moore (Boxford), daughter of Dennison P. and Cynthie P. (Foster) Moore.

Sept. 23.
- Benjamin Victor Conant (Topsfield), son of Benjamin and Margaret (Starrett) Conant.
- Nellie Beatrice Gilland (Salem), daughter of David O. and Lois A. (Hurlburt) Gilland.

Sept. 29.
- Arthur Hanson Furber (North Conway, N. H.), son of Alpheus and Mary Little (Hanson) Furber.
- Charlotte Anne Peabody (Topsfield), daughter of Charles J. and Annie R. (Smith) Peabody.

Dec. 30.
- Willie A. Fuller (Topsfield), son of Timothy and Lydia M. (Peabody) Fuller.
- Grace E. Pierce (Salem), daughter of John S. and Eva L. (Gilbert) Pierce.

DEATHS.

1903.

Feb. 20. Ruth Permelia, wife of Samuel Conley, and dau. of Eleazer and Hannah (Gould) Lake, aged 52 yrs. 1 mo. 26 dys.

Feb. 21. Florence May, wife of Manuel Frederick Castle, and dau. of Clarence Leland and Julia Macbeth (Wotton) Brown, aged 17 yrs 9 mos. 20 dys.

Mar. 5. Mary Ann, widow of William Henry Skinner, and dau. of Edward and Sally (Henfield) Downing, aged 66 yrs. 10 mos. 26 dys.

Mar. 10. John Lynch, son of Thomas and Hannah (Callahan) Lynch, aged 87 yrs. 9 mos. 10 dys.

27. Moses Dorman Pike, son of Benjamin and Huldah (Dorman) Pike, aged 53 yrs. 2 mos. 7 dys.

May 27. Lillian May Lake, dau. of William G. and Margaret (Walker) Lake, aged 12 yrs. 10 mos. 11 dys.

DEATHS (Continued.)

July	9.	Louisa L., wife of Benjamin P. Hobson, and dau. of Jacob T. and Elizabeth (Banks) Strangman, aged 58 yrs. 7 mos. 12 dys.
Aug.	20.	Mary Lane, wife of William Webster Gallup, and dau. of David and Adeline (Lane) Story, aged 67 yrs. 11 mos. 20 dys.
Aug.	29.	Merriam E., widow of George Rideout, and dau. of Oliver and Mary (Maddox) Lowell, aged 73 yrs. 3 mos.
Oct.	12.	Alpheus A. Gould, son of Andrew and Mary P. (Lake) Gould, aged 57 yrs. 6 mos. 4 dys.
Oct.	16.	Ellen Perry, widow of Edward B. Pierson, and dau. of Justus and Hannah (Wood) Perry, aged 76 yrs. 3 mos. 29 dys.
Dec.	9.	Harriette Myrtle Taylor, dau. of Ormond Curtis and Elizabeth (Carnes) Taylor, aged 4 yrs. 6 mos. 19 dys.
Dec.	29.	Mary Osgood, widow of John Hodges, and dau. of Thorndike and Mehitable (Batchelder) Deland, aged 95 yrs. 21 dys.
Dec.	30.	Ira Perley Long, son of Henry and Catherine (Perley) Long, aged 46 yrs. 10 mos. 10 dys.

Deaths in other places, interment in Topsfield.

1903.

Jan.	3.	Elizabeth Pratt, died at Springfield, Mass., aged 69 yrs.
Feb.	2.	Mary E. Patch, died at Danvers, Mass., aged 67 yrs. 7 mos. 18 dys.
April	27.	Bessie M. Fuller, died at Chicopee, Mass., aged 22 yrs. 4 mos. 28 dys.
May	8.	Chester R. Kneeland, died at Salem, Mass., aged 10 yrs. 9 mos. 11 dys.
July	27.	—— —— Fuller, died at Danvers, Mass., aged 4 mos. 16 dys.
Aug.	3.	Emily Bradstreet, died at Salem, Mass., aged 64 yrs. 9 mos.
Aug.	10.	Ella J. Fuller, died at Danvers, Mass., aged 3 mos. 7 dys.
Sept.	17.	Harland H. Wildes, died at Portland, Me., aged 33 yrs.
Oct.	27.	Elizabeth H. Rust, died at Salem, Mass., aged 84 yrs. 4 mos. 15 dys.
Nov.	11.	Agnes Q. McLoud, died at Boston, Mass., aged 53 yrs. 11 mos. 7 dys.
Dec.	9.	Ann E. Hammond, died at Boston, Mass., aged 85 yrs. 6 mos. 7 dys.
Dec.	9.	Carolyn B. McLaughlin, died at Boxford, Mass., aged 31 yrs. 4 mos. 19 dys.

[Oct. 12, 1903, Lewis Bixby, died at Medfield Insane Asylum, aged about 50.]

CHRONOLOGY OF EVENTS IN TOPSFIELD IN 1903.

Feb. 21. Stanwood Church Home for children closed.
Apr. 8. Rev. H. William Hook appointed pastor of the Methodist church.
June   Heavy rains. River very high.
Aug.   Arthur D. Wiggin, of Troy, Vt., elected principal of the High school.
Oct. 12. Alpheus A. Gould killed by a train at Towne's crossing.

BUILDINGS CONSTRUCTED DURING THE YEAR 1903.

Porter B. Peabody, Summer street, dwelling-house and barn.
Benjamin Lane, Main street, Kimball's store remodeled into a dwelling-house.
Benjamin Lane, Central street, the Benjamin Poole house remodeled and raised to two stories.
C. Harry Shoemaker, Ipswich street, house remodeled, addition built; barn remodeled; carriage-house moved and made into a dwelling-house.
Arthur U. Hutchings, Main street, large addition to barn; also a silo.

HOUSES TORN DOWN, 1902-1904.

David Pingree, Garden street, old Red House, so called, 1902.
J. Morris Meredith, Cross street, small dwelling-house, 1903.
Lester E. Libby, River street, old David Balch house, 1904.
David Pingree, small dwelling-house at the corner of Salem and Hill streets, 1904.

VITAL STATISTICS OF TOPSFIELD, MASS.,

FOR THE YEAR 1904.

BIRTHS.

1904.
Feb. 5. Ralph Otis, son of Frank Ezra and Julia Agnes (Bushey) Gould.
Feb. 26. John Francis, son of Albert Herman and Josie (Tinkham) Davison.
Mar. 27. Lewis Kemble, son of Harland S. and Maud (Fuller) Pierce.
June 16. ———— ————, dau. of Daniel Joseph and Katherine Louise (Gibney) Kerrigan.
July 4. John Rogers, son of Hazen Rogers and Mary Elizabeth (Deickhoff) Wildes.
July 29. Warren Dudley, son of Forrest Warren and Alice Lillian (Perkins) Rust.
Aug. 11. Herbert Lansin, son of Fred Ensley and Harriet Ellen (Fuller) Watson.
Aug. 27. Albert William, son of Thomas James and Florence Anna (Pierce) Luxton.
Nov. 12. Henric, son of Pietro and Maria Clotilde (Rossi) Giovannacci.
Nov. 23. Mary, dau. of Harry Gray and Maude Elizabeth (Brackett) Welch.
Dec. 8. Alice Elizabeth, dau. of Archer and Elizabeth Helen (Merry) Andrews
Dec. 23. ———— ————, son of Arthur Freeman and Leonie (Cruchet) Perkins.

MARRIAGES.

1904.
Feb. 24. { Forrest Warren Rust (Topsfield), son of Loring A. and Mary A. C. (Towne) Rust.
Alice Lillian Perkins (Topsfield), dau. of Josiah P. and Phebe W. (Towle) Perkins. }

Mar. 12. { Roy C. Maxwell (Topsfield), son of William Henry and Mary Margaret (Brown) Maxwell.
Elizabeth Gertrude (Beal) Barnard (Topsfield), dau. of Levi L. and Alice L. (Crowdis) Beal. }

MARRIAGES (Continued.)

April 2.
- Edward F. Hill (Lynn), son of Henry and Margaret (Miles) Hill.
- Nellie F. (Clark) Lawler (Lynn), dau. of Charles H. and Addie A. (Andrews) Clark.

April 14.
- Wilmot Allan Watson (Topsfield), son of Ansley and Mary (Wolverton) Watson.
- Clara W. Collins (N. Danville, N. H.), dau. of Oren E. and Flora M. (Webster) Collins.

April 20.
- Charles L. Elliott, Jr. (Danvers), son of Charles L. and Myra (Trask) Elliott.
- Edna M. Hutchins (Leeds Junct., Me.), dau. of James and Cornelia (Hutchins) Hutchins.

June 20.
- C. Harry Shoemaker (Topsfield), son of George Y. and Harriet (Vansant) Shoemaker.
- Fanny Dewey Gray (Boston), dau. of Joseph H. and Maria L. (Dewey) Gray.

June 20.
- Timothy Jesse Fuller (Topsfield), son of Timothy and Lydia Maria (Peabody) Fuller.
- Edith Alma Smith (Greenfield, Mass.), dau. of George and Adeline Dwight (Corey) Smith.

Aug. 2.
- Charles William Stark (Topsfield), son of Joachim and Frederika (Stark) Stark.
- Minnie Myrtle Latham (Marlborough, Mass.), dau. of Stephen B. and Nancy E. (Bond) Latham.

Oct. 6.
- Leone Parker Welch (Topsfield), son of William and Ellen Augusta (Hood) Welch.
- Mary Adaline Smith (Topsfield), dau. of Augustus Willard and Harriet Bartlett (Shaw) Smith.

Oct. 9.
- Mack Charles Henley (Topsfield), son of Charles and Emma (Wesel) Henley.
- Mary Elizabeth Burke (Topsfield), dau. of John T. and Mary J. (Lonsby) Burke.

Oct. 18.
- Emery Wilder Goodwin (Peabody), son of James C. and Bertha A. (Hicks) Goodwin.
- Lucy Josephine Tarbox (Topsfield), dau. of Samuel W. R. and Rosa A. (Dezell) Tarbox.

Nov. 19.
- Harry M. French (Boston), son of Charles H. and Mary A. (French) French.
- Alice M. Wildes (Boston), dau. of Solomon and Anna M. (Harding) Wildes.

VITAL STATISTICS FOR 1904.

DEATHS.

1904.
Jan. 29. James Cotton, son of Samuel and Phebe (Blethen) Cotton, aged 87 yrs. 7 mos. 5 days.
Feb. 12. Frances M. MacCormack, dau. of John R. and Bertha E. (Mellish) MacCormack, aged 2 yrs. 2 mos. 13 dys.
May 7. Eben Jewett Hobson, son of Prescot and Dorothy (Jewett) Hobson, aged 77 yrs. 13 dys.
June 13. Rebecca Emily, widow of John Blaisdell, and dau. of Daniel and Rebecca (Pratt) Hoyt, aged 73 yrs. 2 mos. 24 dys.
June 16. Harriet Elizabeth, wife of Daniel Alvin Conant, and dau. of Nathaniel and Grace (——) Peck, aged 61 yrs. 9 mos. 6 dys.
Sept. 9. Betsey, widow of McKenneth McLeod, and dau. of Thomas and Emma (——) Maxwell, aged 86 yrs.
Sept. 24. Bertha Milson, wife of William Ladd Dodge, and dau. of Lewis Cass and Esther (Rogers) Milson, aged 56 yrs. 2 mos. 9 dys.
Oct. 30. Eliza Mary, widow of Benjamin Fuller, and dau. of Cummings and Lydia (Fuller) Foster, aged 74 yrs. 8 mos. 18 dys.
Dec. 6. Elizabeth Phillips, dau. of Richard and Jane (Talbot) Phillips, aged 87 yrs. 27 dys.
Dec. 6. Lydia Ann, widow of David S. Lane, and dau. of Fitts and —— —— Elwell, aged 93 yrs. 11 mos.
Dec. 20. Alfred Cummings, son of William and Sarah (Scott) Cummings, aged 80 yrs. 6 mos. 23 dys.
Dec. 31. Benjamin Conant, son of John and Ruth (Stanley) Conant, aged 69 yrs. 2 dys.

Deaths in other places, interment in Topsfield.

1904.
Feb. 10. Harriet Emerson, died at Boston, Mass., aged 38 yrs. 4 mos. 14 dys.
Mar. 10. Elizabeth C. Floyd, died at Danvers, Mass., aged 72 yrs.
Mar. 15. Susan Peabody, died at Waltham, Mass., aged 79 yrs.
July 27. Jeremiah Balch, died at Waltham, Mass., aged 81 yrs. 2 mos.
Dec. 5. Harriet S. Porter, died at Hyde Park, Mass., aged 55 yrs. 10 mos. 5 d.

CHRONOLOGY OF EVENTS IN TOPSFIELD IN 1904.

        Much snow fell during the winter of 1903-4.
May 8. The Asa Bixby house, on Rowley street, destroyed by fire.
June 12. The David Granville Perkins house, on Central street, destroyed by fire, also a carriage-house and a shed.
Sept. An appropriation from the Mass. Highway Commission expended upon Central street.
Nov. 8. John L. Fiske, of Topsfield, elected representative to the General Court
Nov. 9. Ell of the Benjamin Conant house, on Rowley Bridge street, destroyed by fire.

BUILDINGS CONSTRUCTED DURING THE YEAR 1904.

Thomas E. Proctor, Perkins street, dwelling-house remodeled; cottage house built; also carriage-house, machine shop, and engine house.
David Pingree, Hill street, mansion house, porter's lodge, and stable.
Richard Wheatland, off Cross street, dwelling-house and stable.
Arthur H. Wellman, off Salem street, dwelling-house and stable.
Harris E. Perkins, Central street, dwelling-house.
Henry B. Williams, Main street, dwelling-house, the old house moved to Rowley street.
Connolly Bros., Rowley street, dwelling-house moved from Main street to Rowley street and remodeled.
William H. Niles, High street, house moved to top of hill and remodeled with additions.
Willard Emery, Main street, new stable built and old stable remodeled.
Joseph B. Poor, Grove street, grain house.
Howard Ford, Pine street, barn.
I. M. Woodbury, Summer street, coal office.

INDEX

TOPSFIELD HISTORICAL COLLECTIONS
VOLUMES I-X.

Accident at barn raising (1784), iii, 5.
Adams, Capt. John G. B., Address at the 250th Anniversary, vi, 78.
Allen, Justin, M. D., Biographical sketch of Dr. Royal A. Merriam, iv, 120.
    Introductory remarks at the first regular meeting of the Topsfield Historical Society, i, 1.
    Some account of Toppesfield, Eng., vi, 133.
Anniversary, Celebration of 250th, of incorporation of Topsfield, ills., vi, 1.
Appleton, Gen. Francis H., Address at the 250th Anniversary, vi, 91.
Averill family, The cradle of the, ii, 84.
Balch, Benjamin J., Topsfield Warren Blues, ills., i, 19.
    Franklin, Charles H. Holmes, lawyer and poet, ii, 88.
Bangs, Gay Esty, Isaac Esty and some of his descendants, v, 105.
Baptismal records of the church in Topsfield (1727-1841), i, pt. 2; ii, pt. 2.
Barnes, Rev. H. B., Register of St. Margaret's, Toppesfield, Eng., x, 1.
Bates, Hon. John L., Address at the 250th Anniversary, vi, 64.

Bi-Centennial Chorus in 1850, vi, 148.
Births in Topsfield, 1643-1850, ix, 1.
Bradstreet, Anne, her life and works, ills., i, 3.
  Dudley, farm for sale in 1835, v, 40.
  Elizabeth Porter, Trial of for the crime of arson, i, 30.
  Metta, Anna Bradstreet, her life and works, ills., i, 3.
  Moses, Obituary notice, v, 136.
  S. Gertrude, The cradle of the Averill family, ii, 84.
Boardman, Capt. Daniel, Obituary notice, v, 139.
Boardman family in Topsfield, ills., viii, 102.
Breck, Rev. Daniel, Some account of, vi, 137.
Boxford, List of inhabitants who took the oath of allegience in 1677-8, iii, 46.
  Town records, 1685-1706, v, 41.
Boyd-Peabody-Waters house on Salem street, Some account of, ills., x, 86.
Buildings constructed during 1900, vi, 156.
  Constructed during 1901, vii, 144.
  Constructed during 1902, viii, 132.
  Constructed during 1903, x, 140.
  Constructed during 1904, x, 144.
Bunker Hill Battle, Mention of, v, 130.
California journals and correspondence of David Lake, iii, 154.
Capen, Rev. Joseph, Funeral elegy on the death of John Foster, ii, 82.
  Some account of, vi, 50.
Celebration, July 4, 1826, vi, 150.
Cemetery inscriptions, Cummings burying-ground, v, 131.
  Lake burying-ground, x, 90.
  Lower cemetery, vii, 107.
  Pine Grove, vii, 1.
  South Side, v, 117.
Church records, baptisms (1727-1841) i, pt. 2; ii, pt. 2.
Clark, Marietta, and others, Isaac Cummings and some of his descendants, ills., v, 1.
  Howletts and Clarks, ii, 53.
  Howlett mills, with some account of the Hobbs' family, iii, 165.
  Note on Samuel S. McKenzie, ii, 112.

INDEX. 147

Clarke, Dan, Petition in 1758, v, 126.
Clarks, The Howletts and, ii, 53.
Cleaveland, Rev. John, Elegy on the death of Benjamin Kimball, x, 68.
   Nehemiah, Some account of Toppesfield, Eng., vi, 130.
     Sketch of, i, 35,
"Colleges," Some account of the, ii, 84; viii, 49.
Conant, Albert A., Address at the 250th Anniversary, vi, 81.
   George, Some account of, iv, 40.
Copper Mines in Topsfield, ii, 73.
Court records relating to Topsfield (1642-1658), v, 143.
Cummings burying-ground inscriptions, v, 131.
   Isaac, and some of his descendants, ills., v, 1.
   Rev. Joseph, Note on, vi, 146.
   W. F., and others, Isaac Cummings and some of his descendants, ills., v, 1.
Cummins, Judge David, portrait, v, 1.
Deaths in Topsfield (1643-1850), ix, 1.
Deaths in Topsfield (1658-1800), iii, 101.
Deeds relating to early settlers, vi, 149
Dennis, Rev. Rodney Gove, Some account of, vi, 144.
Donaldson, George C., Cummings burying-ground inscriptions, v, 131.
Dow, Mrs. Ada B., Centennial hymn, vi, 9.
   George Francis, Baptismal Records of the Church in Topsfield (1727-1841), i, pt. 2; ii, pt. 2.
     Court records relating to Topsfield, (1642-1658), v, 143.
     Deaths in Topsfield (1658-1800), iii, 101.
     Historical address at the 250th Anniversary, vi, 37.
     Letters from a gold hunter, iii, 154.
     Newspaper items relating to Topsfield (1770-1815), iii, 1; v, 132; x, 98.
     Pine Grove cemetery inscriptions, vii, 1.
     Settlement of Topsfield, i, 15.
     Topsfield town clerk's records (1659-1698), ii, 1; iii, 53.
     And others, Isaac Cummings and some of his descendants, ills., v, 1.
Drowning accident at Hood's pond (1792), iii, 12.
Elegy on the death of Benjamin Kimball, x, 68.
   On the death of John Foster (1681), ii, 82.

Emerson, Rev. John, Obituary notice (1774), iii, 3.
Esty, Isaac, and some of his descendants, v, 105.
  Mary, some account of, v, 108.
Fires, Burning of the Rea tavern, i, 7.
  In Topsfield, viii, 70.
Fiske, Amos Tenny, Biographical sketch of, ii, xii.
Fort, Some account of a, viii, 5.
Foster, Edwin O., Address at the 250th Anniversary, vi, 93.
Fourth of July Celebration, 1826, vi, 150.
Gardner, Augustus P., Address at the 250th Anniversary, vi, 86.
Gilbert, Rev. Thomas, Some account of, vi, 47.
Glazier, Mrs., Clarissa, Historical sketch of the Methodist church in Topsfield, ills., iii, 24.
Gleason, Rev. George L., Reminiscent address at the Topsfield Academy reunion, iv, 97.
Gould, Dr. Humphrey, Reminiscences of Rev. Asahel Huntington, x, 78.
  Lieut. John, The treason of, iii, 174.
  John H., portrait, i, frontispiece.
Greenleaf, Benjamin, Some account of, iv, 27.
Haven, Mrs. Theodore W., Trial of Elizabeth Porter Bradstreet for the crime of arson, i, 30.
Healey, Joseph, Some account of, iv, 43.
Herrick, Capt. Nehemiah, Revolutionary service of, v, 127.
Hobart, Rev. Jeremiah, Some account of, vi, 49.
Hobbs family, Some account of, iii, 165.
Holmes, Charles H., lawyer and poet, ills., ii, 88.
Hotel, Topsfield, for sale (1835), iv, 148.
  Some account of, viii, 19.
Houses and buildings in Topsfield, ills., viii, 1.
Howlett mill and the Hobbs family, iii, 165.
Howletts and Clarks, The, ii, 53.
Huntington, Rev. Asahel, Reminiscences of, x, 78.
  Some account of, vi, 140.
Indians, Mention regarding, v, 129.
Kimball, Benjamin, Elegy on the death of, x, 68.
  Jacob, Topsfield, a hymn composed by, vi, 10.
Lake burying-ground inscriptions, x, 90.
  David, California journals and correspondence of, iii, 154.

INDEX. 149

Leach, Mrs. Louisa (Morgan), Biographical Sketch of, ii, xi.
    The burning of the Rea tavern, i, 7.
Letters from a gold hunter, iii, 154.
Lexington, Battle of, mentioned, v, 129.
    Battle of, see also Revolutionary War.
Library, Town, Some account of, iii, 43.
Lodge, Hon. Henry Cabot, Address at the 250th Anniversary, vi, 60.
Lower cemetery inscriptions, vii, 107.
Map of localities near Topsfield village, iv, 76.
Marriages in Topsfield, 1643-1850, ix, 1.
McKenzie, Alfred, The McKenzie family in Topsfield, ii, 106.
    Samuel S., Some account of, ii, 112.
McLoud, Rev. Anson, Life and work of, port., iii, 37.
Meeting-house of 1759, Some account of, vii, 90.
    Seating in the, vii, 90.
    Some account of, iv, 146.
    Some account of old, viii, 15, 38.
Merriam, John, M. D., Some account of, iv, 121.
    Royal A., M. D., Biographical sketch of, port., iv, 120.
Methodist church, Historical sketch of, ills., iii, 24.
    Some account of, viii, 7.
Meyer, George von L., Address at the 250th Anniversary, vi, 90.
Militia, Topsfield Warren Blues, ills., i, 19.
    Training-band notice (1774), iii, 4.
Mills, The Howlett mill, iii, 165.
    Francis Peabody's grist mill, ills., i, 39.
    Some account of, viii, 23, 26, 49.
Moody, Hon. William H., Address at the 250th Anniversary, vi, 31, 88.
Moore, Rev. A. W., Anniversary sermon, vi, 13.
New Meadows, Deed of land in 1642, v, 143.
Newspaper items relating to Topsfield (1770-1815), iii, 1; v, 132; x, 98.
Noyes, Joseph Hale, Some account of, iv, 35.
Oak tree, Old, vii, 105.
Oath of allegiance and fidelity. List of those who took the oath in 1677-8, iii, 46.
Peabody-Batchelder-Young house off North street, Some account of, ills., x, 84.

Peabody, Charles J., Address at the 250th Anniversary, vi, 71.
  Sketch of Dr. Nehemiah Cleaveland, i, 35.
 Francis, grist mill, ills., i, 39.
 Will and inventory of his estate, 1698, x, 91.
 Helen E., The life and work of Rev. Anson McLoud, port., iii, 37.
 John jr., Letter written by, in 1811, x, 81.
 Nathaniel, Biographial sketch of, port., vii, 35.
 Seth, Patriotic song composed by, x, 88.
Peabody-Waters house on Salem street, Some account of, ills., x, 86.
Perkins, Rev. George H., Address at 250th Anniversary, vi, 27.
 John W., Address at Topsfield Academy reunion, iv, 81.
  Address at the 250th Anniversary, vi, 83.
 Rev. William, Some account of, vi, 46.
Perley, M. V. B., History of the Topsfield Academy, ills., iv, 1.
 Sidney, Boxford town records, 1685-1706, v, 41.
  The oath of allegience and fidelity in 1677, iii, 46.
  Topsfield Village in 1800, ills., vii, 124.
Petition from Ipswich farmers (1758), i, 18.
Philbrick, Eliza, Note on Rev. Joseph Cummings, vi, 146.
Pike, Baxter P., Address at the 250th Anniversary, vi, 29.
Pine Grove cemetery inscriptions, vii, 1.
Poole, Rev. Francis A., Address at the 250th Anniversary, vi, 75.
 The treason of Lieut. John Gould, iii, 174.
Pray, Ruel Benton, Biographical sketch of, ii, xi.
Rantoul, Robert S., Address at the 250th Anniversary, vi, 73.
Rea tavern, Burning of, i, 7.
Revolutionary War. Ammunition used by Topsfield men at the Concord fight, vii, 140.
 Notes regarding, v, 127.
 Records regarding, x, 83.
 Topsfield minute men at the Battle of Lexington, i, 10.
Roads, Communication regarding (1801), v, 134.
Schofield, George A., Address at the 250th Anniversary, vi, 68.
School-houses, Some account of, viii, 5, 25, 38, 47, 59, 63.

Searle, Anna, Some account of, iv, 24.
Seating in the meeting-house, vii, 90.
Smith, Joseph F. jr., Asahel Smith and some account of the Smith family, viii, 87.
Smith family letters, x, 74.
Song composed by Seth Peabody, x, 88.
South Side cemetery inscriptions, v, 117.
Streets and roads in Topsfield, viii, 2.
Sunday observance in 1796, iii, 18.
Taverns, Petition of Dan Clarke, 1758, v, 126.
Tax list in 1668, iii, 51.
    In 1725, iii, 49.
Tax of 1798, United States Direct, vii, 57.
Tax payers in 1663, Delinquent, vii, 56.
Toppesfield, Eng., Register of baptisms, marriages, and burials, at St. Margarets', ills., x, 1.
    Some account of, vi, 107.
Topsfield, Early deed, ills., vi, 41.
  Early ministers at, vi, 39.
  Early settlers, Deeds relating to, vi, 149.
  Hymn composed by Jacob Kimball, 1793, vi, 10.
  In 1828, vii, 54.
  In 1836, vii, 55.
  Settlement and naming of, vi, 38.
  Settlement of, i, 15.
  Settlement of, Records in relation to, ii, 1.
  Town clerk's records (1659-1698), ii, 1; iii, 53.
  Village in 1800, ills., vii, 124.
  Warren Blues, ills., i, 19.
Topsfield, Maine, Some account of, vi, 106.
Topsfield Academy, History of, with account of the reunion in 1897, ills., iv, 1.
Topsfield Historical Society, Constitutions and list of members (1895), i, v.
    Introductory remarks at the first regular meeting of the, By Justin Allen, M. D., i, 1.
    Secretary's report (1895), i, vii.
    Secretary's report (1896), ii, vii.
    Secretary's report (1898), iv, v.

Towne, Mrs. Abbie W., The Topsfield copper mines, ii, 73.
    William Towne, his daughters, and the witchcraft delusion, i, 12.
    And others, Isaac Cummings and some of his descendants, ills., v, 1.
    Annie F., Francis Peabody's will and inventory of his estate, 1698, x, 91.
    George W., South Side cemetery inscriptions, v, 117.
    H. Rose, The Boardman family in Topsfield, viii, 102.
    John H., The Boyd-Peabody-Waters house, ills., x, 86.
    The Peabody-Batchelder-Young house, ills., x, 84.
    Francis Peabody's grist mill, ills., i, 39.
    Topsfield houses and buildings, ills., viii, 1.
Town Hall, Some account of, viii, 38.
Town meeting proceedings (1773), iii, 2.
Treason of Lieut. John Gould, iii, 174.
Tree, Old oak, vii, 105.
Trial of Elizabeth Porter Bradstreet for the crime of arson, i, 30.
Turnpike, Newburyport and Boston, Some account of, v, 139-142.
United States direct tax of 1798, vii, 57.
Vital records of Topsfield, 1643-1850, ix, 1.
    Records for 1900, vi, 153.
    Records for 1901, vii, 141.
    Records for 1902, viii, 129.
    Records for 1903, x, 140.
    Records for 1904, x, 144.
Vose, Francis, Some account of, iv, 16.
Wilkins, Jesse A., Some account of, iv, 37.
Witchcraft, William Towne, his daughters, and the witchcraft delusion, i, 12.

CPSIA information can be obtained
at www.ICGtesting.com
Printed in the USA
BVHW041000180119
538188BV00006B/90/P